Never be on the brink!

Ans:

....

"*On the Brink* is an entertaining and insightful read for leaders as you join corporate anthropologist and consultant Andi Simon in participative observation through seven real business cases. She helps both readers and leaders see with fresh eyes: Finding new opportunities, solving stagnant problems, and working with a company's culture as the key to what you see, do, and achieve."

—Marcella Bremer, co-founder of *OCAI-Online* and *Leadership and Change Blog*

"*On the Brink* is a must read for any leader who wants to remain relevant in this fast-changing world. Written in plain English, combining how-to with real-life stories, Andi Simon teaches us to open our minds, go exploring, watch, listen, and discover the opportunities hidden at the core of our business."

—Elisa K. Spain, leadership coach and Vistage master chair

"Every CEO knows they need to see the world through a fresh perspective, but most are wondering where that perspective can be found. In *On the Brink* Andi Simon shows us that the perspective we're seeking can be found when we look at the world from the eyes of our customers."

—Luke Hohmann, CEO, Conteneo, Inc.

"The business world is constantly evolving, and the companies that thrive are the ones that evolve with it. Through the innovative practice of corporate anthropology, Andi Simon has created a framework and set of techniques that any enterprise can use to adapt to changing times and be ready with their next big idea."

—David Warnock, founder and senior partner, Camden Partners

"Every leader should pick up a copy of *On the Brink*. It's a must-have resource, especially in this time of transformative, customer-led change."

—Phil Terry, CEO, Collaborative Gain

"*On the Brink* takes the mystery out of corporate anthropology and its practical impact on business challenges. Whether the issue at hand is developing or iterating on strategy or resolving general organizational design challenges, Andi breaks down the model and methods into practical steps that ensure every company understands its customers, how their needs are changing and/or evolving, and how to harness a company, and its culture, around those needs to ensure long-term growth and success."

—Jamie Candee, president and CEO, Questar Assessment, Inc.

"Andi's perspective and voice are original and come from a deep understanding of corporate anthropological techniques and years of working with companies struggling to find new answers to the old question of how to grow their business in an ever-rapidly changing environment. The book is a must-read for businesses looking to differentiate themselves, create value, and thrive. Andi is a master at breaking down the complex and varied options businesses face into a clear cohesive strategy, brand, and set of implementation tactics—a rare combination of talents."

—Carmen Effron, founder and CEO of C F Effron Company

ع

ON THE BRINK

BRINK

A FRESH LENS TO TAKE YOUR
BUSINESS TO NEW HEIGHTS

ANDI SIMON, PhD

GREENLEAF
BOOK GROUP PRESS

This publication is designed to provide accurate and authoritative information in regard to the subject matter covered. It is sold with the understanding that the publisher and author are not engaged in rendering professional services. If advice or other expert assistance is required, the services of a competent professional should be sought.

Published by Greenleaf Book Group Press
Austin, Texas
www.gbgpress.com

Distributed by Greenleaf Book Group

For ordering information or special discounts for bulk purchases, please contact Greenleaf Book Group at PO Box 91869, Austin, TX 78709, 512.891.6100.

Design and composition by Greenleaf Book Group and Sheila Parr
Cover design by Greenleaf Book Group and Sheila Parr
Cover image © iStockphoto.com / Enis Aksoy

Cataloging-in-Publication data is available.

ISBN: 978-1-62634-280-4

eBook ISBN: 978-1-62634-281-1

Part of the Tree Neutral® program, which offsets the number of trees consumed in the production and printing of this book by taking proactive steps, such as planting trees in direct proportion to the number of trees used: www.treeneutral.com

TreeNeutral®

Printed in the United States of America on acid-free paper

17 18 19 20 21   10 9 8 7 6 5 4 3 2

First Edition

THIS BOOK IS DEDICATED TO ALL OF MY
WONDERFUL CLIENTS WHO WERE ON THE
BRINK AND LET ME HELP THEM SOAR.

CONTENTS

INTRODUCTION

What Is Corporate Anthropology and What Can It Do for You?

IF THE WORD "anthropologist" makes you think of Margaret Mead writing about young people coming of age in Samoa, that's not a bad place to start. Anthropology is defined as the study of human society—language, symbols and shared stories, values and beliefs. Traditionally, it has been applied to distinct cultural groups—often in exotic settings—such as islanders, Native Americans, or other tribal members. Yet, over the past half-century, anthropologists have employed their theories, methods, and tool kits closer to home to study cultures in manufacturing plants, among consumers, and even in business settings.

Corporate anthropology is an extension of traditional anthropology that is used in non-traditional, modern settings. By looking at a company as a new and unfamiliar culture—all the while using techniques that anthropologists use—it's possible to arrive at fresh insights that can help companies sustain their growth and adapt to changing environments. Corporate anthropology is the key to seeing a business problem in an original light or finding previously unimagined opportunities; a key to avoid remaining stuck by reverting to old habits, old solutions, or old cultures.

In the last few years, well-known corporations have found corporate anthropology instrumental in various ways. Google hired an anthropologist to help it better understand the meaning of mobile technologies. Intel has anthropologists on its staff, and at times the company has even engaged external anthropologists to bring new perspectives to its in-house team. In one instance in particular, the external group was engaged to study and better understand how people of various socioeconomic groups use technology in their daily lives. Intel also applies the anthropological method to its strategic development to empower its people to practice—quite simply—better business thinking.

Similarly, ReD, a successful research firm based in New York and Copenhagen, specializes in applying the anthropological method to analysis of its clients' customers. While conducting research for Absolut Vodka, ReD's charge was to study how people consume vodka and other liquors. To focus on the emotional nuances of the social setting in which people share alcoholic drinks, ReD's team observed people at parties. What they found was that what mattered most to partygoers and their hosts were the stories that accompanied the libations. They saw people sharing personal anecdotes in which certain brands of liquor played a memorable role in, say, a vacation. Extrapolating from that, ReD was able to suggest innovative ways the Absolut brand could fill that role in a proprietary and profitable way.

Another well-known case study concerns Samsung. Engineers and executives at the company assumed that TVs should have large screens in order to deliver pictures with superior resolution to customers. Little did they know—until corporate anthropologists pointed it out—that people actually thought of

TVs as part of their home décor. The reason they wanted larger screens was because those looked better in their living rooms or entertainment centers. Samsung's engineers retooled their products accordingly, paying special attention to how they fit into a variety of living spaces rather than merely to how they performed on technical spec sheets.

This is precisely what corporate anthropologists do. We see the things that are really happening out there in the field, not what business leaders *think* is going on. We look for the deeper meaning in the interactions that make up people's lives and the objects they surround themselves with. We search for those cultural symbols that people live by but have a hard time telling you about. And then we use our findings to help companies rethink how, and why, they're doing things.

From 2000–2015, the *Harvard Business Review* and *The New York Times* each ran a series of articles about why businesses should hire anthropologists and should do so immediately. These articles all shared a common theme: how to grow or change by hiring anthropologists to study your business's culture.

Others were urging business schools to add anthropological training to student education. Grant McCracken, the author, anthropologist, and blogger, once advocated a business school course on anthropology and ethnography in business. He believed it would reveal how people inside and outside a company or organization really think and feel, and how culture influences what they desire—even when there is no rational reason for desiring those particular things. This course, McCracken suggested, would also help them see how to use these methods for their business careers to develop products, pursue innovation, and uncover new and often big markets.[1]

Four Key Areas Where Anthropology Really Works

Broadly, what are some of the issues that anthropology can address, and what insights can it offer through its concepts and methods?

1. Anthropology can be used to diagnose and change a company's culture.

   Why is this important? For one thing, management and employees alike can get so comfortable with their way of doing things that they can't see new solutions to old problems or new opportunities to grow and prosper. Understanding a company's culture (and reflecting on it and sometimes worrying about it) should be the concern of every CEO, manager, and department head, not just the concern of the organizational development or human relations folks. All too often, however, executives really don't know much about their corporate culture. It is typically referred to as "the way we have always done things here." The way a company has always done things is not a very useful concept when it comes to assessing if that way works in new business environments or changing technology and business processes.

2. Anthropology can help rethink and communicate a corporate strategy.

   Corporate strategy is a simple story that helps organize where a company is going and how it thinks it should get there. Companies don't always have a clear strategy, and even if they do, it may not be shared beyond the boardroom or the C-suite. In fact, the lack of a clear strategy might be what took a struggling company into the challenges it is facing today. Part of understanding and changing a company's culture often means moving leaders to rethink where the company or organization needs to head in the future and then finding new ways to communicate that direction throughout the organization. What you say and how you live that message must be aligned in an organization.

3. Anthropological methods can be used in concept development, product design, and new business evaluation.

Ethnography and other anthropological tools allow you to see how people in their daily lives solve problems, get things done, and give meaning to their lives. For that reason, these methods have been particularly valuable to the research that goes into product design and market development. Consumers may not really know what they think about a product; in a focus group or a survey, they often tell you what they think you want to know. But when you watch them actually solve problems, use your products, and go through their daily lives, you can see the gap between what they say and what they do. To really find out what they think and need (and what they may not be able to verbalize), you have to participate with them, observe them, and listen to their stories. Research can also help you kill a product when it no longer meets the needs or the customer has found a better alternative.

4. Anthropological methods are valuable to branding, marketing, and sales.

The entire arena of branding and marketing is changing. Inbound sales are challenging the traditional methods of developing leads and closing sales. When anthropologists focus on trends—in micro-communities as well as the culture at large—they can uncover new ways for companies to build brand value, engage with prospects, build relationships with customers, and sustain growth in innovative ways. What users and consumers are saying about you to each other in social media is invaluable and can lead to great innovation when continuously applied in an ongoing stream of episodes.

Why I Wrote This Book, and What I Hope Readers Will Learn

It's important to realize that when my clients hired me, they weren't looking for an anthropologist. They wanted someone to help them solve business problems—falling sales, lack of growth, outdated strategy, or aggressive competition—in a businesslike way. Thanks to my worldview, which had been shaped by my training as an anthropologist, I was able to lead them to notice solutions and opportunities that were actually right in front of them. It was their own aha! moments that ultimately led to breakthroughs in their businesses.

How each client in my various cases arrived at their aha! moment made for compelling stories that illuminate common challenges that businesses face today. The case studies also demonstrate the variety of anthropological tools that the CEOs and I have used to confront and overcome those challenges.

It occurred to me that I wanted to share those insights and methods with the widest possible audience, because, while there are very good reasons to hire professionally trained anthropologists to do observational research for you, there are many tools executives can try themselves. In fact, as I've worked with clients in a collaborative effort, many of them have become very good amateur anthropologists. Once our clients began to see what we do and how to do it, they embraced the methods and tools themselves.

My point, though, is not for you to change careers. It's to help you understand and use anthropological tools and methods to open your eyes to new opportunities—even in fast-changing and difficult times—and achieve greater success than you may ever have dreamed possible.

Who Is Andrea Simon?

You might be wondering how I became involved in this field. My initial expertise was in academia. I started out like so many college students who fall in love with anthropology. I attended Pennsylvania State University to complete my undergraduate courses. I then went on to earn a PhD in anthropology from the City University of New York, and became a tenured professor in the Anthropology and American Studies program at Ramapo College in New Jersey. Eventually, I was invited to teach entrepreneurship to arts and science students as a visiting professor at Washington University in St. Louis.

As an academic, I did several Master Lecture series and produced two educational television *Sunrise Semesters* for CBS. Meanwhile, I was fascinated with understanding how people adapt to new environments, whether they were immigrants from Greece (among whom I did my research) coming to live in New York or Greeks in New York returning to their homeland to spend summers in their village. Their cultural and behavioral changes were obvious to me, though they would quickly tell me that they were simply adapting to their different environments to thrive.

At one point my career took a sudden turn. My interest and experience in how people change led me to be introduced to Citibankers, who were transforming the culture of banking as the industry was being deregulated. I became a consultant for them for a year and I worked on moving the staff's culture from one where employees simply attended work to one where they became top performers.

It didn't take a lot for me to eventually shift my focus and go into the business of using the anthropological concepts, methods, and tools I had relied on in academia to help companies change. I thrive on change, so how could I continue to follow the same path for my whole life? But change is not necessarily easy, and here I was moving from a very comfortable environment at the university—where I had predictability and tenure and understood what the expectations were—to an entirely new environment. I felt a bit like those immigrants I had studied. And I, like them, realized I had to adapt my behaviors and join the culture of corporate banks in order to thrive.

For two decades, I was a senior executive with financial services and health-care institutions. Whether it was one commercial bank merging with another, a savings bank trying to become a commercial bank, or a health-care system trying to survive with managed care, I saw that the challenges were basically the same: The times were changing, and neither organizations nor their staff knew quite what to do. It was clear to me that I liked to actively help organizations adapt and change; I didn't want to just stand back and watch them go through the challenge of doing so.

Since founding my own firm in 2002, I've worked with dozens of companies through webinars, workshops, and individual consulting to help them overcome the challenges of operating in fast-changing environments. When we launched Simon Associates Management Consultants, we did so as corporate anthropologists focused on helping organizations change. The benefits of using anthropological methods and tools quickly became evident as I applied them to a wide variety of business and nonprofit settings.

The common denominator among my clients has been the extreme difficulty with which CEOs react to changing circumstances—a challenge that requires seeing, feeling, and thinking in new ways. As a consequence, many of their businesses have stalled. They no longer know how to serve and help their customers. It's a rare CEO who doesn't fall into this category; Steve Jobs of Apple was a notable exception. He often looked beyond the obvious. He trusted his tech designers, and above all, he trusted himself—more than he trusted consumers or researchers. "It isn't the consumers' job to know what they want," he famously said. And as Henry Ford observed years earlier, "If I had asked people how to improve their transportation, they would have told me to make their horses go faster."

But there *are* ways to figure out customers' actual pain points and to come up with innovative solutions to deal with them, and that's where corporate anthropology can make a difference. What's more, it can help companies avoid the dreaded stall point or a corporate crisis brought on by the terrifying realization that the world is changing and the firm cannot keep up.

Over the years, there were many lessons learned and lots to share. As we observed organizations and listened to their staffs, we realized that ideas were coming from many different places, but the ideas weren't being heard. In many companies, the best ideas come not just from CEOs but also from employees, customers, and partners. The real challenge for leaders is to create a place where these ideas can come together and turn into innovations. One way to create this place is by encouraging leaders to step outside their daily routines and observe how unspoken human behaviors and habits can turn into big ideas that impact corporate success.

My response to those who might say that only trained anthropologists should use anthropological methods is: Why would we hold back on any resource that can help leaders take their businesses, their staff, and their products in new directions to foster and sustain growth? These are directions that will build long-term value for stockholders, stakeholders, and employees. As Martha Stewart says, "That's a good thing."

1 Berkun, Scott, "How to Win by Studying Culture: An Interview with Grant McCracken," *Harvard Business Review*, August 18, 2008. https://hbr.org/2008/08/how-to-win-by-studying-culture.html.

··

CHAPTER 1

ACRES OF DIAMONDS

WHEN SIMON ASSOCIATES Management Consultants were introduced to TELERx Marketing Inc. ("TELERx") in 2008, Linda Schellenger had just become the president of that subsidiary of Merck & Co., Inc., Kenilworth, New Jersey, USA. The company was a leading contact center outsourcer specializing in customer care for the consumer package goods and health-care industries. It had experienced a period of limited growth and had lost three requests for proposals.

Schellenger and her management team were perplexed by changes transforming the customer care industry and how to best tackle them to regain their leadership position. She was looking for a fresh approach to take TELERx to the next stage in its business. With revenues at about ninety million dollars, there seemed to be a broad scope of opportunities, albeit with an abundance of competitors. What could they do to energize clients, add innovative services, and generate new revenue streams?

Founded in 1980, TELERx had begun with innovative marketing techniques that harnessed the cost-effectiveness of telephones to deliver critical communications to clients' customers: doctors, nurses, and pharmacists. Over the next fifteen years it had expanded into the compliance arena and then was able to leverage its experience and expertise to other industries.

In 1994, TELERx became a wholly owned, independent sub-sidiary of Merck & Co., Inc., Kenilworth, New Jersey, USA.

To probe what had stalled the company's growth, we began by spending time with their call center staff, listening to calls coming into TELERx and learning about what issues they weren't able to resolve for the inbound callers. As we listened, we began to wonder about the caller profiles. Were they older or younger? Were they calling with common problems or unique ones?

> MUCH OF WHAT JUMPED OUT
> AT US WAS UNEXPECTED.

Much of what jumped out at us was unexpected: Most of the callers were over the age of fifty. They used to write inquiry letters but had switched to the telephone. Younger people, however, didn't use the telephone to obtain information. Gen Y and even many Gen Xers were relying on text messaging and online solutions. Younger people were turning to corporate websites, online forums, or texts to friends and family to find answers. Clients hadn't paid much attention to this demographic shift.

We could see that emerging trends were going to impact the customer care experience: Blogging and Facebook were opening up strong new avenues to engage with customers. The question was: Should TELERx be driving its clients' business or waiting for the clients to ask for these solutions? Could it shift the clients' focus and offer service options that could build engagement and reduce problems or simplify solutions?

We worked with the team on broader strategy, beginning with a two-day retreat. The goal was to help them see what the company was investing in and how that investment compared with the competition in the industry.

What the team saw was a commoditized industry where price was becoming the key driver of choice. Since TELERx was a higher-priced service provider that believed in a comparable higher quality for its US-based telephone centers, it was going to be hard to demonstrate better value to prospective clients who were being driven to lower-cost solutions abroad. And for those who felt it was easier to control the costs and the quality of in-house call centers, the value of an outsourced solution was going to be a challenge.

The team could see how the business was being challenged, but it still was not sure where to go to differentiate it, refocus it, or grow it.

So the next step was to send them out exploring to better understand how people were thinking about customer care. They concentrated on four areas:

- Some called on prospective clients who had not outsourced their customer care services to TELERx. The idea was to let the prospects talk about what they were doing, find out where their problems or unmet needs might be, and listen to the stories they were telling about how their current solutions were working—or weren't.

- Others went to major companies that had a relationship with Merck—customers, noncustomers, and pharmaceutical companies.

- Still others attended conferences and spent time at colleges to see what younger people were actually doing to solve their customer care challenges.

- Finally, some team members talked to current clients to see what they were doing, what they needed, and what they might be missing.

What did *the team* learn?

First, the companies that had not selected TELERx to manage their customer care services had, by and large, kept their customer care solutions inside. These firms had decided to continue to provide an 800 number for their internal call center solutions. It wasn't a matter of selecting one outsourced solution over another. It was about how they thought they should best offer customer care to their customers—from inside or outside.

What could TELERx offer companies *who* wanted to keep their solutions inside?

TELERx was an expert in telephone customer care centers but was not selling that expertise as something another company could leverage or learn from. And its excellent technology and system support could possibly become revenue streams for companies that didn't want to outsource customer care but did need expertise and systems experience.

Second, the team found out that major companies were consolidating customer care centers after acquisitions or were beginning to look at customer care in a broader context—online solutions, for example. Others were rethinking customer care solutions as revenue opportunities instead of expenses.

Could TELERx help lead those transformations? What value could it offer in innovative ways?

Third, the research among younger generations who had grown up digital offered some really big ideas. What mix of channels were people using? A typical website even in 2008 had an 800 number along with chat capabilities, frequently asked questions, a link to social media, such as a Facebook page, and a forum.

People were also going to sites to find out about drugs, how to take and use them properly, their contraindications, and so forth.

How could TELERx offer the expertise to help people manage their care and help drug companies ensure better compliance and safe use?

Finally, current clients presented the most perplexing questions. One team member pointed out that TELERx was collecting data that their clients were not currently accessing. Could TELERx turn that data into information and insights that it could sell back to the clients? Could TELERx become a source of expertise by finding trends and helping their clients respond to them?

In response to these findings, the TELERx team began to expand their vision beyond telephone call center solutions, as they realized the scope of potential revenue and growth opportunities. The solutions were there waiting for them, but the big ideas had come from the process of exploration, from listening to their prospects and clients talk about their needs—both met and unmet—and from sharing the information in a systematic manner.

In addition, it was a time of team building where everyone from the telephone operators to the senior leadership could see how their insights could help frame the strategic direction of the company. Realizing that those calling into the center were older adults was an aha! moment that led us to look at how younger people behaved. And seeing what they were doing led us to think about what TELERx could do for its customers today.

Why Are We So Blind?

Why was it that Schellenger and her team couldn't see the opportunities by themselves? For that matter, why do most of us miss what's right in front of us? The answer can be summed up in a famous lecture given by Russell Herman Conwell, an American

Baptist minister best remembered as the founder and first president of Temple University in Philadelphia in the 1880s. Conwell's stirring lecture, called "Acres of Diamonds," begins with an ancient Persian tale of a wealthy but dissatisfied farmer who sells his farm and travels the world in search of a diamond mine. The farmer's search is fruitless, and he dies many years later in poverty. Meanwhile, the man who buys the farmer's land finds a shiny black rock in the stream that runs through the property. The rock is a diamond, and, as the new owner discovers, the farm is littered with the gems. The once-disparaged property becomes one of the most lucrative diamond mines in the world and its jewels decorate the crowns of monarchs.

The moral of the story? If the Persian farmer had bothered to explore his own holdings, he would have found acres of diamonds—instead of wretchedness, poverty, and death.

Conwell goes on to give several other examples of men who can't see the riches that are in front of their noses. Through his stories of wealth-seekers and their failures, Conwell hammers home his point: For virtually any business, the opportunities you are looking for are very possibly right in your own backyard. "I care not what your profession or occupation in life may be," said Conwell. "I care not whether you are a lawyer, a doctor, a housekeeper, teacher, or whatever else, the principle is precisely the same. We must know what the world needs first and then invest ourselves to supply that need, and success is almost certain."

IT NEVER CEASES TO AMAZE ME HOW MANY BUSINESS LEADERS FAIL TO RECOGNIZE THAT THEY'RE SITTING ON ACRES OF DIAMONDS OF UNMET NEEDS OR OBVIOUS FUTURE OPPORTUNITIES.

In my own work as a corporate anthropologist, it never ceases to amaze me how many business leaders fail to recognize that they're sitting on acres of diamonds of unmet needs or obvious future opportunities. It's not that these executives are bad managers or inept. It's just that they can't seem to see what is right in front of them.

So where are these gems? Maybe they're buried in customers' emails asking for services they're not sure the company provides. Or they're unnoticed at a business's call center where operators tell inquirers, "No, we don't make that." Often great ideas come from employees who see better ways to do things but can't seem to find a champion who will give their ideas a chance. Why is that? The company's collective brain and its culture are getting in the way.

The Problem Lies in the Brain

The first question is: Why don't we see something? The answer is the brain simply puts up obstacles.

Two of my favorite quotes capture the challenge neatly: Marcel Proust said, "The only real voyage of discovery consists not in seeing new landscapes, but in having new eyes, in seeing the universe with the eyes of another, of hundreds of others, in seeing the hundreds of universes that each of them sees."

Similarly, Anaïs Nin wrote in *Seduction of the Minotaur* that the problem is that "we don't see the world as it is; we see the world as we are."

They got it: It is all about our brain.

Now that the neurosciences are finally able to look at how the brain works by using functional MRIs, what we are learning confirms some of our earlier assumptions and contradicts or turns others upside down. We now know that we are born with a brain full of potential. Then, as we grow up, we form perceptual mind maps and stories in our brain that help craft our reality. Once those stories and mind maps are in place, we tend to see the world through that lens, no matter what new information comes in. We sort what is going on around us—including those business opportunities and unmet needs—and only recognize those that fit our perceptions and stories.

> AS HUMANS WE HAPPILY HATE TO CHANGE. WE SIMPLY CANNOT SEE THE UNFAMILIAR, BECAUSE OUR BRAINS ARE ALWAYS TRYING TO FIT WHAT WE SEE AND HEAR INTO WHAT WE THINK SHOULD BE THERE.

Our limited vision and perceptual bias have everything to do with why we see such a constrained reality. As humans we happily hate to change. We simply cannot see the unfamiliar, because our brains are always trying to fit what we see and hear into what *we think* should be there. Not only that—the brain actually creates a chemical reaction when it is learning something new. It normally uses a whopping twenty-five percent of the body's energy; when we're trying to learn something new, it has to work extra hard, expending even more energy.

Haven't you experienced this? When tackling a new computer program, say, or learning a foreign language, or producing a new product, you have to concentrate really hard until the unfamiliar becomes a well-established habit. Until then, your brain literally creates chemical pain that says, "Please stop all that new work. It hurts." Hence, rather than enjoying the challenges that come with the unknown or the untried, we fight change. To be sure, our brains are elastic and can, in fact, change and adapt, but it's not a smooth, easy, or comfortable process. It takes a lot of work.

Returning to business examples, when companies stall, the people running them have to work really hard to alter old thought and action patterns in their quest for renewed success. The question is: How do they (or you) overcome that resistance to see, feel, and think in new ways so that their acres of diamonds are not disregarded or destroyed?

As anthropologists, we suggest you give your brain a hand. Your brain is going to fight you. So you need a willingness to embrace change, to listen with different ears, and to see with new eyes—*even if it's painful*. Often that means a taking a good look at a company's culture.

It Is All About Culture

Ever since the time of cavemen, people have formed cultures, which are a shared set of core values, beliefs, and behaviors. It's part of what makes us human. Companies have cultures too, whether they know it or not, because companies are made up of people. A company's culture is an amalgam of its core values, beliefs, and behaviors that pertain to the business and the way it is conducted. Employees live out that culture every day. People join or remain in companies where they feel most comfortable, and they eventually develop habits that make their work go as smoothly as possible.

Anthropologists and others working in corporate settings realized quite early that cultures can help a company match the challenges of a competitive environment or cause a mismatch that threatens a company's viability. These cultures don't just happen. They have to be intentional, designed with an understanding of how those values, beliefs, and behaviors—along with the symbols and rituals that support them—fit specific business challenges.

Yet, of course, times change. The demographics of employees change, too. Employees grow up and become comfortable in their roles and the way things are. When corporate cultures have to evolve, communicating that fact to those who work in the business can be a challenge.

Seeing with fresh eyes, assessing reality, and changing a company's culture can be difficult, I admit. But it's not impossible, as you'll see in the case studies that make up Chapters 3–9 of this book. And in a fast-changing business climate, it's often a necessity.

What makes the process possible is applying the concepts, methods, and tools of anthropology. And after many years of working with corporate decision-makers, I have learned how to help them do just that. Once these company leaders see what's really going on, they are then able to rethink how they can successfully respond to the challenges of their business environment.

The point is that you, too, can follow their lead. Let me introduce you to the anthropologist's tool kit.

CHAPTER 2

....

THE ANTHROPOLOGIST'S TOOL KIT

SO, WHERE DO you start? What are these anthropological practices and how do you put them into action, not theoretically but in reality, in your own business? Don't worry. The list that follows is not intended to be a master's program for you. Instead, think of these as easy-to-understand, simple-to-use methods and tools to help you do three important things.

> IT'S IMPORTANT TO GET OUT OF YOUR
> OFFICE AND SYSTEMATICALLY WATCH AND
> LISTEN TO WHAT IS REALLY HAPPENING,
> INSTEAD OF WHAT YOU THINK IS GOING ON
> OR WHAT HAS BEEN GOING ON IN THE PAST.

1. Conduct Observational Research. It's important for you to get out of your office and begin to systematically watch and listen to what is really happening, instead of what you think is going on or what has been going on in the past. Since people (customers or clients) often cannot express

what they are doing, thinking, or believing—or how their culture, core values, beliefs, and habits guide them through their daily lives—you have to watch them and record what you see. This is the core foundation of how anthropologists explore the essence of a culture. Similarly, when the process is applied to companies, you can step back and observe, listen, and participate as an outsider to see the situation in a new way. I contend that this is the best way to uncover what someone may not be able to put into words. By doing so, you will discover

- their challenges,
- the difficulties of having to compete in oversaturated markets with too much supply and diminishing demand,
- the major trends they see approaching that worry them and that they're not prepared for,
- how they could use a hand finding nonusers with unmet needs who could help expand the market, and
- how the cultural differences among generations are changing the traditional ways of doing business.

2. Find Customers' Pain Points. Next, you need to take a good look at all those key points of contact where people are trying to get answers to their questions or solutions to their problems. You may be amazed at their frustrations when they call into your customer service center. Where are email inquiries coming from and what are they asking? What is happening when people visit your website to search for something? Do they stay or abandon you? What if you could see them on video?

3. Use Culture Probes and Storytelling. What are the stories customers or clients could tell you if only they had a chance to share them? There are ways to listen with different ears.

These are the broad goals. Now, specifically, what kinds of things can you do?

First: Go Exploring

The core idea here is that you need to separate yourself from what you typically do in your daily work. To get your customer or noncustomer's perspective, you need to see them actually doing their jobs, solving their problems, and perhaps using your products or services . . . or those of another company. Among other things, you may find that those whom you're observing don't really like the solutions they've come up with, but they may not have any alternatives.

Here are several ways to step out and look around:

SPEND A DAY IN THE LIFE.

Ask a client or customer if you can shadow them. Then follow them throughout their day and watch them do their work. Have lunch in their cafeteria. Stand alongside a production operator. Listen to what challenges them and watch for their pain and pleasure points. When do they give high fives and when do they express frustration or uncertainty?

ENGAGE IN PARTICIPANT OBSERVATION.

Go beyond observing and actually do your client's or their employees' job. You'll be amazed at what you can learn by personally running the machinery, answering the phones, pouring the coffee, or writing copy on deadline. For a model, take a look at TV's *Undercover Boss*. That show demonstrates some of the best participant observation work from a corporate perspective, and it is easily available on YouTube.

You can imagine what people are doing in their jobs, but you really can't know what they are feeling or thinking; nor can you understand the interactions they have inside or outside the company. You can ask them, but they will undoubtedly tell you what they think you want to hear. To get at the reality, listen and try to do their jobs alongside them. You'll begin to see unmet needs and opportunities where you could provide new solutions, open new markets, or institute efficiencies.

DO SOME DEEP HANGING OUT.

Sometimes you cannot follow customers all day or even part of a day, but there is another way to observe subjects in their own environment doing things as they generally do them: You can hang out and watch them use a product or get their jobs done. Say you're a hotel chain, and you want to redesign your properties so they're more comfortable for your guests. Rather than conducting a typical survey, go sit in a lobby and see what guests really do—or don't do.

HANG OUT AND WATCH YOUR CUSTOMERS
USE A PRODUCT OR GET THEIR JOBS DONE.

Marriott did just that, and it turned out that guests wanted better facilities for work meetings, casual relaxation areas, and better food offerings. Those findings became the catalyst for the design of all Marriott Courtyard hotels.

Whether you're observing or participating, there are nuances that you will need to remember.

RECORD WHAT YOU SEE OR SAW.

Always take a notebook with you. After you have a moment to reflect on your time with a client, you need to record your observations. You brain is miserly; it will forget details quickly.

The minute you walk out of the observational situation, write down what you experienced and what you think you noticed. If you can take a video on your phone or turn on a recorder, you can capture even better data. But if you can't, at least be sure you make notes as soon as you are able.

TAKE BREAKS AND THOUGHT WALKS.

To best capture what you are seeing and what you think it means—both to you and to those you are observing—it is important to take breaks and what I call thought walks. This will give you time to reflect upon and analyze what you have observed. In fact, there is a growing body of research that is showing how walking helps us better organize the world around us, enabling the brain to construct better creative solutions to problems and literally change the nature of our thinking. In 2014, Marily Oppezzo and Daniel Schwartz of Stanford University found in their research that "A person's creative output increased by an average of 60 percent when walking."[1]

Remember, the people you are watching are relying on

their habits and are often not consciously aware of what they are doing or how they are doing it. At times when you are in the process of observing them, you may be startled by what you are seeing. You might ask them to explain what is happening, so at least you have their perceptions of their behaviors. Yet you will still be trying to fit the new observations into what you have been pulling together previously. The thought walk may be just what you and your brain need to organize the data points, craft the right narrative or stories about what you are seeing, and understand why it is meaningful to those you are observing and to the discovery process in which you are engaged.

Second: Find Out What's Coming in to You Already

It doesn't matter what type of company you have; prospects often seek you out through different access points—a call center, emails, comments on your website, search results leading to your website, even casual conversations at conferences and networking events. Think of these as your acres of diamonds.

LISTEN IN ON CUSTOMER-SERVICE PHONE CALLS.

What are your customers happy with, mad about, or frustrated by? And how are your customer-service agents responding to their requests, inquiries, and frustrations? Listening to those conversations is an effective way to find out. Are customers requesting something and being told, "No, we don't do that"? Well, why don't you?

FIND OUT WHAT PEOPLE ARE SEARCHING FOR ON YOUR INTERNET SITE.

The new world of inbound marketing provides businesspeople with amazing opportunities to understand who is searching for them, how long visitors stay on their website, and what content they are reading while there. Search data offers immediate insights into people's needs—met and unmet—and how they are trying to meet those needs.

READ YOUR COMPANY'S EMAILS.

Often emails reveal unmet customer needs. One client's emails showed a pattern of inquiries from geographic areas where they assumed there was no demand for their product and, therefore, where the company had no distributors. Would-be customers were finding the company on the Internet and asking to buy their wares.

ANALYZE BLOGS ABOUT YOUR FIELD.

Internet blogs are a valuable source of information about what matters most to the public. There is a wealth of information to be mined if you know where to dig.

Third: Capture the Stories

While observation, documentation, and internal research are crucial tools, you may also want to actively try to understand your customers' inner lives, values, and thoughts—aspects of the culture that they have been reluctant or unable to describe. Anthropologists have effective ways of doing this, and you can follow their lead with the following tools.

CONDUCT LISTENING SESSIONS.

Set up opportunities to listen closely to what your clients are talking about. If you can, go out with your sales team and find out what prospects or customers are saying to your salespeople. Or visit a client and meet with members of the team that you ordinarily don't speak with. If you interact with the engineering staff, then try sales or purchasing, or vice versa. Don't ask questions. Just have them tell you about their business, trends, and things that are challenging for them. Their "what if" questions may actually suggest new possibilities for business.

PROBE THE CULTURE.

Identify a group of key people whom you want to learn more about. These might be current clients, consumers, or employees of particular types of businesses that you need to understand. Give them—individually or in a group—an assortment of objects, such as a diary, a camera, pictures, maps, or books. Then ask them to record specific events, feelings, or interactions. If your observational research is designed to address a problem you are challenged by in your business—let's say it is why your products, kitchen sinks, are not selling well—you might find that people buying and installing those sinks could capture the experience for you and in a far better way than you could do on your own. From their viewpoint, what do they see and how does it feel? Using their phones, they could easily capture some of the key moments that challenge them as they install a new sink in their kitchen. Without much fuss, they could send them to you with their story about what happened and why it didn't match their own expectations. From that image and their narrative you can find out what *they* value and how *they* thought the entire purchase, installation, and use should have happened, and why it didn't meet their expectations. You are looking for the meaning of the experience and the interactions, not just what took place as someone who was renovating his or her kitchen bought a new sink.

As you think about ways to capture the essence of an experience, ask those you are studying to create a visual diary or draft a story about what they have seen or done. These are called culture probes, and they're a way of getting deeper into their perspectives, values, and beliefs about a situation. This will help you analyze their culture, so you can use these insights to design a better product or service that pinpoints your customers' innermost feelings and beliefs.

HOLD STORYTELLING SESSIONS.

Human beings are natural storytellers, and we often use stories to keep tabs on what is happening and to teach others about what is good or bad. Through stories, we practice interacting with others and thereby learn the customs and rules of society. Stories reveal a person's concerns, and they also have a unique power to persuade and motivate because they appeal to our emotions and capacity for empathy.

One of our favorite stories involved a sales manager who went out with one of his salesmen to listen to how he sold their patented foam insulation. He heard the customer repeatedly asking the salesman "What if . . . ?" Those what-ifs were all the things the customer couldn't get done and was hoping the company could help him get done. It was through those stories that the sales manager began to hear what really mattered to the customer, and it opened up real needs in big ways.

With another client, we were out doing observational work on urgent care centers. We kept asking patients to tell us about their experiences. The stories were all about speed, ease, and smiles; not health care per se. Patients said things such as, "Just please take me fast, don't make me sit and wait, and smile a little—like I matter." They expected quality in the doctors, but their experiences at the centers were underwhelming.

USE VIDEO AND PHOTOS.

Pictures are worth a thousand words. Visual tools help you record your observations and then allow you to return to (and confirm) what you've seen and heard. Video or photos can be taken by the subjects themselves, by you, or by an outside team.

There are a number of ways you can start. You can ask people how they do something: how they use your product or solve a problem. Then you can video them actually performing the actions they described. You will see a gap between what they think and what they do. Then ask people what the pictures or photos mean to them. Immediately, you will see how they interpreted the videos or the photos and what you thought you saw in them.

In the early stages of the Internet we would have people tell us how they were going to buy something online. Then we would video them actually doing it. What they said rarely matched what they did. But the video allowed us to better understand both the habits driving their real behavior and the stories they used to tell us what they thought their actions were. The gap opened up a lot of big ideas about how to design better e-commerce experiences.

Wells Fargo sent anthropologists to observe its customers doing their banking. The pictures they took helped the company transform that experience, particularly the online experience.

The Pier 5 Hotel in Baltimore gave its guests cameras and asked them to take photos of their experience in the hotel.

The experiences turned out to be nothing like what the management expected. The photos were all about the fun and ease that parents and children had at the hotel. Management's focus on the business traveler might have been fine during the week, but it completely missed the mark on weekends.[2]

Fourth: Evaluate Your Culture and Perhaps Even Change It

Most companies have a culture, but leaders and employees alike may have a hard time describing it and explaining why it is right for their business model. Nevertheless, it is important to understand what culture is and how it provides the framework for getting business done. To help corporations clarify their culture, we use the method developed by Dr. Kim S. Cameron and Dr. Robert E. Quinn at the University of Michigan. The first step is identifying what kind of culture a business has. There are four types.

1. A Collaborative Clan culture is focused on how people work together to get things accomplished.

2. A Creative Ad-Hoc culture is typical where there is an innovative, visionary entrepreneur who offers an empowering, ad-hoc cultural environment.

3. A Competitive Market-Driven culture is highly focused on results and externally on the competition.

4. A Controlling Hierarchical culture is rules-driven and focused on processes and procedures, controls, and conformity.

For a first step, you can use the Organizational Culture Assessment Instrument (www.ocai-online.com) and see how you come out. Then compare the results to what you would prefer to have in the future. You can begin to think not only about what you are doing but also about the key values, beliefs, and behaviors that you and your employees believe define you. Finally, consider if these are an asset or a liability in changing times. Your conclusions will help you determine whether you need to work on altering your culture as part of your strategy for growth and success.

COMMUNICATION IS A KEY.

Insights, observations, changes in a corporate culture, new products and markets . . . all these elements are important, but for a company to succeed, they must be clearly communicated, first within the corporation, and then to the general public. Every employee should know that change is taking place. This should be followed by the strongest possible branding, not only through traditional means but also increasingly through story-telling in social media.

The Anthropologist's Tool Kit in Action

In the chapters that follow, you'll see how the tools described can be used in the marketplace as I explore the stories of seven distinct mid-market companies. Each had enjoyed growth and success. They were led by entrepreneurs who thought of themselves as innovators. But at some point the enterprises stalled, and no one could figure out why. The leaders were frustrated, and so were the employees, as it became obvious that the old ways simply were no longer working as they had in the past.

As you will see, each company, in its own way, realized it had to adapt to changing times. Using a combination of the techniques I've described in this chapter, and working together, we helped them see their situation through a new lens. Regardless of how they arrived at their eureka moments, once they got there, their view of the world dramatically changed. They discovered needs that hadn't been met, customers they had never tried to reach, markets they had never imagined, and phenomenal growth and success.

Let's see how they did it.

....

1   Wong, May, "Stanford Study Finds Walking Improves Creativity," *Stanford News*, April 24, 2014. http://news.stanford.edu/news/2014/april/walking-vs-sitting-042414.html.

2   Wellner, Alison, "Consumers in the Mist," *Inc.com*, April 1, 2003. http://www.inc.com/magazine/20030401/25306.html.

....

CHAPTER 3

LACLEDE CHAIN MANUFACTURING

IN 2009, JIM RILEY, president and CEO of Laclede Chain Manufacturing Company, was sitting in his corporate offices in St. Louis, pondering the future of his business. Like escape artist Harry Houdini, who famously freed himself from a web of four hundred pounds of chains, leg irons, and padlocks a century earlier, Riley seemed to need some kind of magic trick to get his company out of the seemingly unbreakable stranglehold that was hampering growth.

Eight years earlier, Riley had joined with Bush O'Donnell & Co. to buy the firm from bankrupt Laclede Steel Co. At the time, Laclede Chain, which made chains for tires, hardware, and industrial uses, had about thirty million dollars in revenue and was among the market leaders in the two-hundred-million-dollar chain industry.

Riley, a fifty-year-old Pittsburgh native, had lived in St. Louis since 1978. Since 2001, the soft-spoken, serious Midwesterner, known for his curiosity and innovative thinking, had guided the company to some notable successes. He put his stamp on the company soon after taking the reins. At the time, his strategy for growth seemed simple and smart: Grow market share and profits would follow. Indeed, thanks to some particularly severe winters with heavy snowfall in the early 2000s, Laclede's market share almost doubled. Profits were up as well.

In just four years, Laclede's plant in Maryville, Missouri, with 135,000 square feet of manufacturing and distribution space, was running 24/7, churning out as much chain as the company could handle. Unfortunately, all that production eventually led to some unexpected and disastrous results: Laclede saturated the market, and price pressures were intensifying.

Riley thought he knew what to do. To increase profitability, he focused on margin management, shrinking costs by using imported products from China. Initially, this strategy worked well, too. Business remained strong, particularly in harsh, snowy winters when people were reminded how essential tire chains were. But as Laclede's output peaked and market share increases ground to a halt, the strategy of shrinking costs became less and less effective.

"We went after margins instead of market share," Riley recalled, "and that worked well until we realized that we had stopped growing. I didn't know where to go next. We had good costs, and I was stumped."

By 2008, the company had stalled, and Riley and his team had run out of ideas on how to grow. Things were looking dour.

To make matters worse, the Great Recession hit and hit hard. Devastating virtually all industries, this economic tsunami negated years of Laclede's impressive gains. Like scores of mid-market companies, the firm was held back by too much supply and too little demand.

Laclede's plight was hardly unusual. In any economic climate, eighty-seven percent of Fortune 100 companies stall; often, like Laclede, it is after shifting the focus from revenue growth to margin management.[1]

"I looked around, and we were going downhill fast," Riley said, remembering the bad times of 2008. "We couldn't sell what we were making. So we tried to shrink. We laid off people; we backed off production. And even though we all saw what was happening, we didn't know what to do about it."

A Victim of Its Own Success

The prospect of complete failure was made even more unpleasant by the fact that Laclede Chain Manufacturing Company had been around for more than 150 years. The company's roots can be traced back to 1854, making it the oldest domestic chain manufacturer in America. The business had originated as a blacksmith shop forging hardware for wagon trains heading west across America. The offerings evolved with the times, and by the 1890s, Laclede was selling chain and hardware throughout the country.

The firm grew steadily over the next hundred years, expanding its manufacturing plants and broadening its line of products. In 1984, the firm was purchased by Laclede Steel Company of St. Louis. Between 1987 and 1997, Laclede bought state-of-the-art chain-manufacturing equipment and increased its capacity to produce more than twenty million pounds of chain.

Riley's Eureka Moment

In 2009, Riley, along with other CEOs, attended a "Change Matters" workshop I conducted in St. Louis. I typically open these with a reference to Charles Darwin and the fact that it is not the smartest or the strongest that evolve and thrive, but the most adaptive. This observation sets the stage for helping leaders think about the need for change in their companies in a more positive and receptive way. Rather than using oft-used but outmoded brainstorming sessions that tend to lead nowhere, I work with attendees on taking concrete steps to get a company growing again. A core part of the workshop is how to help them see the opportunities all around them with new eyes.

> SOMETIMES BEING VERY GOOD
> AT SOMETHING CAN ACTUALLY
> HINDER A COMPANY'S ABILITY TO
> RESPOND TO CHANGING TIMES.

Said Riley, "Andrea Simon was talking about finding new market space, reigniting a company's energy, and changing the way your business works." He was intrigued by the notion that corporate culture can stifle innovation. How does that happen? Leaders or employees within a company come to rely on the behaviors, beliefs, and solutions that are comfortable and established, and dislodging them may seem insurmountable. Applying this observation to his own dilemma, Riley realized that being very good at something—selling snow chains—was actually hindering Laclede's ability to respond to changing times. He was energized by the idea that his company could look for new kinds of customers at a time when its core market was mature and stagnant.

After participating in my workshop, Riley went back to his management team and key executives in the three locations where Laclede had operations. "We really had to figure out where else we could start selling chain," said Riley. "At the end of 2009, we had dropped off sixty percent from our prior year's revenue levels. Clearly we didn't have enough sales."

WHAT ARE OUR CUSTOMERS ASKING FOR THAT WE AREN'T SELLING?

He asked the teams for ideas on adapting the company to solve its current business crisis: "What can we do to grow?" "How do we open up sales? How can we sell more *chain*, maybe not just snow chains?" There was one final question, perhaps the most important of all: "*What are our customers asking for that we aren't selling?*"

Then Riley brought the teams together and reviewed their ideas. Ultimately there were several key themes, none of which were that startling, just good business thinking. These themes were

1. create new products,
2. find new customers,
3. develop strategic partners,
4. open government sales, and
5. reorganize the company.

Riley particularly liked the third and fourth suggestions. He freely admits that he never thought of either. But the first breakthrough came with new products, which grew out of requests from customers.

Listening for Opportunity

Riley began to listen to what people were asking for that he and his staff said they didn't provide. In particular, he became aware of customer service calls from people looking for products that Laclede had never tried to offer. Crucial opportunities were being lost as phone reps patiently explained to customers—and potential customers—that they did not sell those types of chains.

"These calls were coming in through our customer service unit, but the operators didn't know how to solve the customers' needs," Riley said. "What was worse was that I wasn't even aware of these calls. Then I started to monitor the calls to our sales department and heard them for myself. I was listening to opportunities that were literally right in front of my nose. We were turning away potential buyers simply because it wasn't our core business. But why? And government? We never thought they would have any need for our snow chains. But by listening in on those calls, I found out that the US government needed *a lot of chain* for all sorts of things."

Giving Customers What They Want

"Hearing those customer inquiries totally changed our entire approach to business," Riley said. "Now we help customers find the things they want. We try never to say no. If a customer needs something, they tell us what they're looking for, and we go find it for them. We discovered that a lot of our distributors were selling things that we weren't and were in markets we weren't in. We asked them to sell to us and to our customers, and we agreed not to compete with each other. Then we created ways to make it easy for us to call them, get a quote, and have them ship directly to our customers."

Part of the overhaul of his company's direction is the new emphasis on innovations by the employees, not just by the CEO or the top executives. "Get your team members to lead the way," Riley said. "And then let them keep going. They will be the energy behind your reinvention."

Laclede's growth was coming from employees' ideas and

the sense of responsibility and empowerment they shared. The employees themselves had ownership of the company's new direction, which has made all the difference. Laclede truly became a solutions provider, not just a chain producer.

> ONCE A COMPANY DEFINES SUCCESS IN A PARTICULAR WAY, ITS EMPLOYEES TELL THAT STORY, THINK THAT WAY, AND WORK TO MAKE THE STORY COME TRUE. BUT WHEN THE STORY STOPS WORKING, YOU NEED A NEW ONE.

In my work with companies that have stalled, I see this all the time. Once a company defines success in a particular way, its employees tell that story, think that way, and work to make the story come true. But when the story stops working, you need a new one. The employees often have great ideas but no way to share them or test them.

"The key to our market troubles was that we didn't think of ourselves as having customers," Riley said. "We sold link chain, which is very different from roller chain. So we didn't sell roller chain or serve customers. When I hooked up with the president of another chain company who was selling to one of our good customers, he became a supplier, and as a result, we both got more business. Even though we were still two suppliers, we quickly realized that *we* is much better than *I*. We stopped competing and started complementing each other. We won, and so did our customers—we gave them competitive pricing and excellent service."

As Laclede's people started to innovate on their own, Riley

also found he didn't have to push people to do new business development or find ways to grow. In one division, employees developed new products and found new customers. In another, they pursued government sales and strategic partnering. In yet another, they reduced costs, lured new customers away from competitors, and discovered new ways to sell more products.

How to Change a Company

Laclede's example opens the question of how best to change a company. Let's assume that people in an organization are willing to change, as long as the right approach is taken. But what is the right approach?

> MOST COMPANY INITIATIVES—
> INSTALLING NEW TECHNOLOGY,
> DOWNSIZING, RESTRUCTURING,
> OR TRYING TO CHANGE CORPORATE
> CULTURE—HAVE LOW SUCCESS RATES.

Extensive research on change management and organizational development reveals that a change process's design and management is crucial to the success or failure of organizational change. And success is still fairly difficult to come by. Most company initiatives—installing new technology, downsizing, restructuring, or trying to change corporate culture—have low success rates. In fact, approximately seventy percent of all change initiatives fail.[2]

Managing change typically works best when it's based on delegation and decentralization while preserving central cohesion. Top-down hierarchical decisions often fail to get employees on board, and success is doomed if the staff is not involved in carrying out changes.

Indeed, what Riley discovered was that there was enormous value in his people, who were a critical source of knowledge and experience. I've found over time that the most effective change comes from a collaborative team effort, led by an entrepreneur or innovator. Riley understood this immediately and applied it with great success.

Equally important is the concept that cultural change in organizations is most successful when there is a pleasant culture in which people feel safe and trusted so they can quiet their minds.[3] This quiet mind is critical, because it allows people to visualize how they can play new roles in an emerging business environment. Fresh ideas then emerge in all kinds of ways.[4]

Throughout the process, the leader and the change manager must maintain the feeling that employees are trusted and that they are important if individuals are going to engage in the game of change. They must help keep the organization focused on where it is going or it becomes very difficult for employees to believe that their ideas will make any difference.[5]

The Importance of a Bold, Curious Leader

In the case of Laclede, Riley recognized very early on that change was as much about his culture and his people as it was about the business. His employees were the key to his future success more than anything else he did. And it was how the people *changed themselves* that made all the difference. They altered their basic approach—their attitudes, values, and most of all their behavior—to doing business at Laclede. Building on the core strengths of the team, Riley's staff quickly realized how people could help each other. They got their co-workers to buy into the new ideas before ever going forward with them. They took responsibility for delivering results, instead of waiting for someone else to make the first move.

As Riley described it, "We encouraged people to work together, and we discouraged arguments among divisions or departments. It was really about the people themselves wanting to do a good job and wanting their company to succeed. We gave everyone rewards for doing things better and getting good results."

A perfect example of Laclede's new culture was illustrated one night when Riley got a phone call from his purchasing/engineering manager, who had just returned from a business trip to China. The manager had a friend in the birdseed business who wanted to produce and market metal birdcages. Suddenly the employee had his own aha! moment: He realized that, in fact, Laclede could manufacture those birdcages for his friend's company.

Before you knew it, Laclede was producing 140,000 birdcages—this was a world apart from making chains for snow tires. On top of that, Laclede realized it could also capitalize on the excess space in their shipping containers loaded with heavy chain, providing a low-cost shipping solution for the birdseed company.

"The most exciting part is that we now employ 152 people, all of whom are part of the new Laclede," boasted Riley. "Ninety-nine are in manufacturing and assembly, and another fifty-three are in sales, engineering, and purchasing. They all have the ability to add to our business through innovations and ideas. We take hourly workers, train them, and listen to their ideas on how to do things. Now it's OK for someone to do something out of the box, and they don't have to wait for me to approve it. And if they make a mistake, they learn from it."

Freedom from Rules

What worked for Laclede can also work for any company. Give your people an opportunity to be successful and they will be, as Riley found. "We had a culture in which rules kept our people from being successful and smothered them," he said. "But it's all different now. Our customers are getting into the act as well. When I'm at an industry convention, competitors will come up to me and encourage me to call them for things I had not thought of before. I now realize that we can sell *with them* instead of thinking we are competing *against them*. I now understand that sharing customers is good for our business and for our customers."

And what has become of Laclede? There's been a chain reaction of success. In 2010, Riley, along with longtime general manager Steve Heuett and a private equity group, bought out the company from Bush O'Donnell. Business jumped forty percent in 2011. Of course, growth is never a straight line. As winters grow warmer and the sale of snow chains becomes more difficult, Laclede has bought their chain manufacturing equipment from China and opened a new facility in Mississippi. Now they are producing Made in USA chains, and they continue to open new markets in unanticipated ways.

Lessons Learned from Laclede for Your Company

You may be wondering: What does this have to do with me and my company? As you step back and take a look at your organization, try reflecting on these four points in Jim Riley's experience and see how they apply to you.

1. ## The most adaptive thrive.
   Laclede's growth stalled due to several forces, particularly a saturated market and effects from the Great Recession. However, the company was also hindered by its 150-year history and a successful core product that stifled innovation and prevented its employees from imagining new solutions to their problems. In order for you to apply corporate anthropology to your company, you must be willing to see your business in a new way. Take a step back from "the way things are" to consider new opportunities and become adaptive to changing times.

2. ## Share corporate anthropology with your team.
   Riley took his lessons on corporate anthropology back to his management team, and you can do the same. Encourage your employees from all levels of the organization to look at your business in a new way and submit new ideas for growth. Corporate anthropology does not work well in a vacuum.

3. ## Listen to learn.
   For Riley, customer service calls were the source of a huge breakthrough in his business. Consider monitoring the incoming calls to your sales or customer service departments and listen for customer inquiries that could represent new business opportunities. You may be surprised by what you hear.

4. Keep communication open and friendly.

Riley recognized that the future success of Laclede relied on his company culture's shifting to one that encouraged trust. Consider rewarding your employees for sharing new ideas, working together, and getting good results, while discouraging cross-departmental arguments and silo-thinking.

....

1 Olson, Matthew, Derek van Bever, and Seth Verry, "When Growth Stalls," *Harvard Business Review,* March 2008.

2 Beer, Michael and Nitin Nohria, "Cracking the Code of Change," *Harvard Business Review,* May 2000.

3 Werkman, Renate A. , "Understanding Failure to Change: A Pluralistic Approach and Five Patterns," *Leadership & Organization Development Journal,* 2009, Vol. 30, no. 7, pp. 664–684.

4 Rock, David, *Quiet Leadership: Six Steps to Transforming Performance at Work,* New York: HarperCollins, 2007.

5 Kotter, John P., *Leading Change,* Boston: Harvard Business School Press, 1996. Ford and Ford, "The Role of Conversations in Producing Intentional Change in Organizations," *The Academy of Management Review,* Vol. 20, no. 3 (July, 1995) pp. 541–570. http://www. professorford.com/wp-content/articles/role.pdf. The research is very compelling concerning dialogue as a form of generating ideas in which all group members can present their ideas and opinions in order to generate insights that individually would be unattainable. (Gustavsen, Bjorn, *Dialogue and Development,* Assen/Maastricht: Van Gorcum and Stockholm: The Swedish Center for Working Life, 1992.)

The underlying assumption is that changing is a collaborative process, effective only if all the players are brought together in a process of exchanging ideas and developing new principles, with every participant's opinion seen as valuable (Senge, Peter M., *The Fifth Discipline: The Art & Practice of The Learning Organization,* New York: Doubleday, 1990, 2006).

....

CHAPTER 4

EAC/INTEGRATED POWER SOLUTIONS

IF ELECTRICITY IS just organized lightning, as comedian George Carlin once said, are batteries just a way of storing lightning in a tube? Certainly, for two decades EAC/Integrated Power Solutions seemed to have no problem keeping sales charged up. The company was a manufacturer that took specifications from clients and built exceptional disposable batteries. But by 2006, founder and president Mark Schmit sensed that something was going wrong. Annual revenue for the Teterboro, New Jersey, company was still around twenty-five million dollars, but growth had stalled. In fact, he was facing his third year without increase in income. Schmit realized something had to change. He had even hired a new sales manager to reenergize revenues, but beyond that, he was powerless to identify the underlying problem.

What had happened to EAC? Schmit was pondering questions like this when I met him at a meeting of the nonprofit board we both served on. For a number of years, Mark and I had worked together on the board of a non-denominational organization that fed the hungry, treated the addicted, and housed the homeless. The organization captured both our passions for giving back to the community, and it seemed to me that Mark had used that sensibility to grow his company—with compassion, teamwork, kindness, and customer engagement.

One day after a board meeting, I happened to ask him if he knew of any companies that needed to change, and I was shocked when he said, "Mine."

EAC/Integrated Power Solutions was a battery design and manufacturing company founded in 1984. As a manufacturer it had more than 175 clients of all sizes—from the military and aerospace industries to oceanographic and seismic surveying, among others. EAC also supplied power solutions for external medical devices such as automated external defibrillators, infusion pumps, patient monitoring devices, and MRI equipment. The firm's expertise was in the design, development, and manufacture of custom battery pack batteries, power supplies, and portable battery systems for a wide variety of applications.

EAC's engineers were experienced and well known for the skill and knowledge they brought to their clients' power requirements. While clients typically came with their engineering specifications already prepared, EAC was exceptional at customizing those specifications in such a way as to ensure that what the client needed was what they actually received, along with the confidence that, once built, those batteries would deliver the power required.

That was why I was startled when Mark asked me to sit down and talk with him and his team about how to expand their business. As we discussed the company, it became clear that EAC really did not sell proprietary batteries or power solutions. It was an outsourced solution provider for customers who needed their expertise to build great batteries. As Mark told me often: "They bring us the design specs, and we build their batteries."

Determined to get EAC on the upswing again, we set to work. My task was to help EAC change, figure out why Schmit's sales team was not really selling, and reignite growth.

We began by analyzing their customer base. Not surprisingly, they followed the 80/20 rule but to a greater extreme: Twenty-two large customers represented ninety percent of his revenue—Thales and the US military among them. But unless these clients grew, or Mark found others like them, EAC would not be able to grow either. The other 150 customers were small and important to EAC's main business, but their requirements were simply inadequate to support major growth projections.

Most importantly, new accounts, the lifeblood of any business, were not coming in through the sales team at all. EAC's six salespeople had all been with the company for many years, but during that time they had stopped going after new clients and instead had become order-taking account managers. Aware of the problem, Schmit had already charged his new sales manager with the task of overhauling the entire process and jump-starting new sales.

Schmit's attention had been focused on improving production and managing his clients. One of his chief initiatives was to build a new factory in China. The current facility was in New Jersey, and as good as it was, EAC was being pressured, both by their clients and by market competition, to reduce its costs. New Jersey was hardly a low-cost manufacturing venue. As a result, Mark and his senior managers had spent a good deal of time overseas looking for a Chinese manufacturing facility, eventually opening one in Suzhou, China, in 2006. He invited us to meet with his suppliers there and see the facility and the staff. Expansion was moving forward quickly. Sales had to catch up.

Getting Out of the Office

From the information that was coming together—the data analysis and the observations—I began to see that it was time to get the EAC team out of its offices. There seemed to be a disconnect between aspects of the business that were important to EAC's management and what industry trends were signifying. Together, we needed to watch how customers were responding to things EAC had invested heavily in, both emotionally and financially.

I took the sales team out to do culture probes and observational research—not only among their clients but also among others. The goal was to get the sales force to listen to people they did not typically deal with—not the folks in purchasing or engineering, but those in R&D and Marketing, C-suite executives, and people on the shop floor who were building the products for which EAC made the batteries.

We were listening for ideas and information about what really mattered to EAC customers—the end-users of the devices powered by its batteries—and also to its nonusers. What was R&D struggling with? What did the CEO of a customer-driven company want to see happen? How were the people in manufacturing dealing with issues? Where were unsolved needs? Where did customers have pain points or headaches? What did they need to work around?

WHEN COMPANIES CANNOT SEEM TO FIGURE OUT WHY THEY HAVE STALLED, CUSTOMERS' PAIN POINTS AND HEADACHES ARE OFTEN GREAT PLACES TO START.

When companies cannot seem to figure out why they have stalled, customers' pain points and headaches are often great places to start. But probing for pain takes a lot of work; at times, EAC sent me out on my own. As it turned out, the non-clients were very interested in our discussions.

EAC clients were all over the United States, so I went with their salespeople wherever there was a client meeting. In Florida, I spent several hours on one client's factory floor. Then I attended meetings with its leadership team, discussing the trends and challenges that were facing them and how they were responding to those challenges. EAC had put a new on-site stocking facility inside this company so they could have just-in-time products without carrying their own inventory. The client was an excellent customer who generously let us observe and listen to the hot buttons and pain points.

Another customer in New England provided time for us to discuss strategies, future product developments, and the role of power solutions in providing them with a real competitive advantage.

Virtually all of EAC's major clients offered us the time to do culture probes, listening for unmet needs that we could begin to develop for them. Rather than wait for them to deliver product specifications, I was looking for what we could do preemptively to offer them value before they even designed their power solutions.

One new client, 3M, came to EAC through the Internet and was already presold on EAC's services. 3M had done its research, had spoken to its suppliers and customers, and came ready to discuss its medical device needs with Schmit. The client invited me out to Minneapolis to discuss EAC and was very candid: Motorola had been supplying the firm's batteries in the past, but was no longer going to be manufacturing the batteries that 3M needed. EAC was very impressive, came with great references, and seemed to have the engineering skills and expertise that 3M was looking for.

It was important for EAC to realize that the Internet was emerging as a powerful force in business-to-business—not just business-to-customer—sales. For EAC's sales team, that thought was unsettling at the very least. None of them had ever thought of calling on 3M, much less expected that company to become a large customer.

This led us to talk with the engineers and sales team at EAC about how they operated. One of the first things I had observed was that EAC's sales team still functioned mainly as order takers. That meant that growth depended on the success of its clients. While an OEM may have sales representatives in the field, new business is often difficult to pry away from a competitor. In this zero-sum game, some OEMs win and some lose, but few really get ahead. The best they can hope for is for a growing economy. As the old adage goes, a rising tide lifts all boats: *If the market is growing, your company can grow as well.* But if a company's market is saturated, it needs to rethink its business strategy altogether.

At the same time, EAC's sales team had turned a deaf ear to increasing requests for chargers. Approximately half of their top twenty clients had at one time or another asked for this product. But EAC typically sent that business elsewhere. Moreover, the salespeople explained to clients that EAC "did not make chargers." Because the company defined itself strictly as an OEM in the battery design and manufacturing business, it had shackled its own growth.

The fact that the industry might be changing did not enter

anyone's mind, and a potentially lucrative core business was being ignored, despite the fact that the market was moving away from disposable batteries to rechargeable ones. In fact, in some of our client meetings the major part of the discussion was about rechargeable possibilities.

Rechargeable batteries and their chargers were not a sidebar. They were becoming essential power options. One client told us that he had batteries that only lasted twelve hours, and he wanted ones that went longer. He hadn't specified longer-life batteries because he didn't know if they were possible. That meant that engineers relied on what they knew, not on what was coming. And they all wanted to know how lithium ion was going to change the power solution options available.

Often, listening sessions focused on clients asking EAC about what it saw as trends in power solutions. EAC was seen as the expert. In one case the customer even wanted to engage EAC in a series of training sessions for their engineers.

As I noted, key themes started to emerge in EAC's comments and those of customers after each session. For example:

- Speed in various forms was important. When pushed, clients said that what they really wanted was for their specs to be turned into models faster. And they wanted ideas to come to them more quickly and easily. Comments about the importance of speed emerged in so many different ways that Schmit was startled that no one had picked up on it before. One client said, "Can't you do it any faster, Mark?" Schmit's response: "You give us the specs, and we build your battery." There was a big disconnect there.

- EAC was considered a thought leader in the field. EAC thought its customers knew all about power and batteries and simply wanted to give the company specs to build power solutions for their products. Actually the clients yearned for EAC to tell them *what it knew about power*, so they could arrive at better designs. It was a fascinating study in divergence. The clients really wanted EAC to be the design expert and to provide better solutions.

- Power solutions provided a competitive advantage. From EAC's perspective, it simply built great batteries to the customer's specifications. But when EAC also created power solutions for the competitor of a customer, the result might be products that surpassed those of the original customer. EAC had never realized that power solutions could provide a competitive advantage. In fact, EAC could take its expertise and give a customer or prospective customer that competitive edge. But corporate culture decreed that wasn't what the company did; it just built batteries to specifications.

- Clients desired EAC's insights. "What is happening in the power industry?" we were continually asked. Clients and non-clients picked our brains at each opportunity. They were very interested in what EAC could do to teach them about innovative power solutions that might help them develop better, faster products . . . now!

- Rechargeable power and smart batteries were the future. Although half of its top clients asked for them, EAC did not make chargers; it blindly handed this business off to others. Why? Again, the company was locked into a narrow definition of itself. But customers were now dictating that battery chargers must be an essential part of the business, not an irrelevant sideline.

- Lighter, longer, stronger power solutions were key. The real need, the biggest headache to solve, was the desire for *lighter, longer, stronger power solutions.* Clients wanted these solutions, and they wanted them urgently.

Overlook Branding and You Overlook Your Business

One other message came through: A strong EAC brand was regarded by the EAC team as unnecessary and totally without value. However, when one of the company's loyal customers took a big piece of business to a major competitor, EAC got a much-needed kick in the pants, which forced it to rethink the value of brands even in B2B enterprises.

One CEO, a customer, put it another way. He had been telling Schmit about his imminent retirement, and Schmit responded that this would have no impact on the customer and its relationship with EAC. Instead, the customer said, almost as a warning, "You *should* be concerned. Whoever takes over my job is going to have his favorite manufacturer. You haven't built a strong brand. I think you are a great battery design company to work with. But will they?"

BRANDING IS NOT AN AFTERTHOUGHT; IT IS VERY MUCH *THE* THOUGHT.

For EAC, the discussion about branding was the most difficult to understand. We had long discussions as I tried to convince EAC that branding wasn't an afterthought; it was very much *the* thought. Unless a company has a strong brand reputation of being a leader in the field—a reputation that others recognize—it risks being easily replaced by another option that seems equally proficient. Branding ensures that a company trusts its outsourced solution providers, based on years of ongoing relationships. But new people have their own trusted providers, and so lack of branding presents a liability. For EAC, this could have spelled its eventual demise. There were many ways to start the branding process. Why, for example, hadn't EAC created the equivalent of the Intel Inside campaign, so that an EAC battery was the preferred provider of power solutions for everyone?

That Aha! Moment

Happily, EAC acted on the insights that we heard as we worked in the field. It wasn't easy but, like Scrooge in Dickens's *A Christmas Carol*, EAC eventually heeded the warnings of past, present, and future and took on a new persona. Schmit rebranded the company as an integrated power solution provider with a focus on being the leader in innovative, integrated power solutions that included those rechargeable batteries. What's more, EAC took steps to position itself as a thought leader in the field and one that could provide a competitive advantage to corporate customers. These strategic decisions made EAC a very desirable acquisition, causing it to be purchased in 2007 for twelve million dollars by Electrochem Commercial Power, a much larger battery company.

What Did We Learn, and What Can You Learn?

How could a company like EAC let itself get into a stall? There was a large market of untapped opportunities in front of it. In addition, clients were voicing their concerns and actually asking for solutions that EAC discarded, but the company was not hearing them. Without the systematic observation of corporate anthropology, the EAC story might have ended quite differently.

Here is how Tom Davenport, author of *Big Data at Work*, championed the benefits of systematic observation:

> It's the key to knowing what's working and what isn't, how people are using technology and other tools in the course of the workday, how workers extract meaning (or don't) from their work, and so forth . . . Corporate anthropology provides the possibility of actually knowing what's happening and why in organizations. Of course, it's not easy. Anthropologists can be a pain in the butt. They will want to watch for a long time before coming to a conclusion—longer than you will deem reasonable. They will question your fundamental assumptions. They will insist on interpreting every little thing.[1]

When it came to uncovering real needs, no one at EAC had ever asked its customers about their struggles and headaches. The idea that they had expertise beyond making batteries to clients' specs was unsettling to them. The concept of a consultative role seemed disconnected from EAC's basic business model of building a battery design for nothing and making money on manufacturing it. It's worth noting that EAC's worldview and culture had both positive and negative results. Clearly the focus on quality had produced an impressive customer list, but that single-minded dedication to simply doing what had always been done had led it to ignore changing customer needs.

> CLIENTS WERE VOICING THEIR CONCERNS AND ACTUALLY ASKING FOR SOLUTIONS, BUT THE COMPANY WAS NOT HEARING THEM.

Blind spots are hardly unusual in business (or in life). Sometimes we realize that something is happening, but we discount the news, ignore it, or consider it an aberration. Case in point: While I was working with EAC, one of its competitors bought a major charger company. That competitor clearly saw value in the fully integrated power solution that a charger company could offer clients in the future. The acquisition was a wake-up call, but not one strong enough to drive EAC to action.

Similarly, the environmental movement was putting pressure on battery manufacturers to replace disposables with rechargeable batteries, but EAC dismissed this trend as unimportant to them. Yet another opportunity lost.

Eventually Schmit and his team recognized that much of what EAC was doing was grounded in past practices and historical experience. Despite the quality product it turned out, times were changing, and clients were changing. EAC had to change, too.

> THE FUTURE, AND FUTURE SUCCESS, BELONG TO THOSE WHO DARE TO CHALLENGE THEIR PAST HABITS AND LOOK AROUND THEM THROUGH A CLEAR NEW LENS OF REALITY.

Living in the past can blind us to reality more than we might imagine. The future, and future success, belong to those who dare to challenge their past habits and look around them through a clear new lens of reality. Mark Schmit reenergized his battery company, and anyone can follow his example.

Lessons Learned from EAC/Integrated Power Solutions for Your Company

How could you avoid Mark Schmit's challenges and learn from his story? Even when I speak with Mark today, we reflect on four things that could help others, perhaps even you.

1. Times are changing. Why didn't I see it?

   It's important, though maybe difficult, to train yourself to see the new as good for you. Business environments are always in flux, subject to disruptive innovations that threaten to negate your solutions. Schmit's story is all about how the times were changing, and yet he repeatedly denied the relevance. Are you doing the same? Instead, turn those coming trends into big possibilities and figure out how you can capitalize on them—not discount them.

2. Go exploring.

   When was the last time you hung out with a client? Sounds like it's time for you and your team to go exploring. No longer can you imagine what is happening in the world your customers are dealing with. Go watch them and see what might be good for your company to capitalize upon.

3. Outliers might be your next big customers.

   Schmit kept discounting requests for charging solutions.

Who is asking you for things about which your team says: "Nope, that isn't what we do"? Do not ditch those outliers! If you stalwartly stick to your core competencies and focus wholly on today's customer, you will miss the future customers coming to you now. Look at those outliers and go meet with them to see how they can become big customers.

4. Sales channels are changing.

Customers were finding EAC via the Internet in 2007, very early in e-commerce's development. Their sales representatives were stunned—no one had ever thought of 3M as a potential customer. With buyers' practices going through a great transformation today, how are you retooling your sales strategy, the skills of your sales team, and the intersections of your marketing, inbound marketing, and sales platforms? You must take advantage of how the new buyer—consumer or business—searches for, evaluates, and buys solutions. Those old cold-calling techniques are yesterday's news.

1   Davenport, Tom, "The Rise of Corporate Anthropology," *Harvard Business Review* (blog), November 28, 2007.

....

CHAPTER 5

A MIDWESTERN
MEDICAL CENTER

BACK IN 2006, I came to work as a consultant at a medical center in the Midwest whose financial prognosis was dire. The $360-million-teaching and safety-net hospital with over four hundred beds had posted a multiyear cumulative loss in excess of twenty million dollars and, like the community where it was located, it was ailing greatly. It faced a real challenge.

I had extensive experience working in and with health-care institutions. In 1996, before I came to this medical center, I set up the branding and marketing at Montefiore Medical Center in the Bronx, New York. And from 1999 to 2001, I worked at St. Joseph's Regional Medical Center, as vice president of branding and marketing. This safety-net hospital, with all of its challenges, was a particularly interesting client for Simon Associates and for me.

I became aware of this medical center through a friend and colleague just as the center was turning around. I was brought on board for branding and marketing support and to do some regional market research. The team at the center was looking for someone to help them better understand their institution's brand positioning (which would be essential if they were to reinvigorate the hospital's growth); to change the organization and rebrand it for a changing market; and to work on its internal branding to provide the staff with a strong new identity. After that, the team wanted to work on altering the medical center's very hierarchical culture. With the changes coming in health-care reform, they knew that the institution had to become more innovative and responsive to the needs of the region.

Turning the center around operationally was a tough job for the management team, many of whom had been there for their entire careers. They had a difficult time imagining how to do *anything* differently, and figuring out how to position the center with two other major medical centers in the area was not going to be easy either. This medical center had been cast as the place to go for those who were poor, very sick, injured, or without many options. Located in what was one of the poorest cities in the United States at that time, the center was an essential safety-net health-care provider for the large Medicaid and uninsured population in the area.

Changing the way the market saw this medical center was going to require some clever communication and marketing, and curing its financial woes meant expanding the patient mix to include many more of those who had health-care insurance.

As I began to design the project, we had to ask: What did the community really think about its medical center? Would the quality of care and the experience and expertise of the physicians and the hospital shift the area residents' feelings about where they could go for care? Since people tend to go where they feel they belong, could we create a new mind-set that suggested that this particular center was their own?

I was asked to run the marketing, branding, and physician services area as an interim senior vice president until the right management talent could be found. I would be doing research using anthropological tools and then managing the department that had to use that research to build the new brand and market the services to the physician and patient communities. It was a very unusual arrangement that turned into four years of a robust—and very special—consultancy.

The Context

This medical center was, and still is, a municipal hospital owned by a city that has endured deep economic depression since the late 1980s. But the hospital hadn't received funding from the city since the early 1970s, and it got no state or federal funds either. In 2008, the center was losing close to twenty million dollars annually. As the team began to address the center's financial problems, great strides were made with the physicians and the other staff. Union employees agreed to ask for no salary increases and began to pay for part of their own health-care costs. Slowly and with great pain, the medical center became revenue positive and cost efficient without diluting its patient care.

By 2009, the center had an operating surplus of one percent, approximately $3.6 million. (The standard for a healthy hospital is an operating surplus of four percent.) The turnaround had begun, but there was still a long way to go before it would become a stable, high-quality medical center that could attract the region's insured population.

One of the strengths that the center did have was its connection to its citizens, who remembered the hospital's history intertwined with their own. Touted as the first local modern hospital, the center had opened with forty beds back in 1908. Two multi-story towers replaced the original building in 1928 and created a 432-bed hospital boasting the most up-to-date diagnostic, surgical, and medical equipment then available.

The 1960s and early 1970s marked the height of the city's prosperity and population, as well as that of the center, which became a financially independent institution in the early 1970s, serving a city that had grown to close to 190,000 residents. However, hard times soon lay ahead. As local employment fell, the city's population dropped almost by half.

By the time I began to work at the center, the community's original four hospitals had combined into three; one moved out to serve the suburbs and the county, and the other was part of a larger health system and was the place to go for those who were insured.

Along with being the standalone, safety-net hospital, the center where I was working was also a very high-level medical center with a Level I Trauma Center, a Burn Center, and a Level III Neonatal Intensive Care Unit, as well as facilities for high-risk pregnant mothers. The pediatric program was exceptional and recognized as such. If your child was sick or injured, the center was the place to go. The numbers attested to the needs: In 2008, it had sixteen hundred trauma cases, one thousand neonatal patients, and ninety thousand emergency room visits.

As for the physicians, seventy-five percent were foreign-born doctors, many from India and Pakistan, reflecting the ethnic complexity of the region. Their varied cultures and their different roles within the hospital affected how they, the nurses, and the staff interacted with each other and with the patients and their families.

Our task was to turn this complexity into a message that would capture the hearts and minds of the community in a way that could shift patients away from other hospitals. With established patterns of referral, this was not going to be easy. But, as we quickly learned, there were lots of great stories to work with. For example, wherever I traveled, I found people who had been born at this particular center; after many years, they still felt proud to be alums and were still engaged with the institution, whether they thought they should go there as adult patients or not.

Observational Research

Doing observational research meant that I had to fit into the community and look at the medical center as the residents of its city did. Because I was commuting from New York, I took a room in a Marriott and spent a few days every week at the center for the first year, and again from 2010 to 2012.

To begin the process, we carried out observations and conducted interviews in the hospital and the community, focusing on perceptions of the medical center as it was and as what people thought it was becoming. Everyone, it seemed, had ideas they wanted to share. By this time, the medical center was emerging from its financial distress. Yet for those who worked there, the times didn't really seem to be changing.

> DOING OBSERVATIONAL RESEARCH MEANS FITTING INTO THE COMMUNITY.

There were many places to observe the 2,500 staff members going through their daily paces. Often I spent time in the lobby, watching the flow of people, listening to their conversations, and observing how they were coping. At other times, I hung out in the cafeteria and asked folks to sit down and talk. It was easy for them to express their feelings, concerns, and ideas and a wonderful way for me to learn about what mattered to them and how change was going to affect them.

Another of my favorite venues was the monthly staff meeting, where the presentations and the staff reactions offered insights into what was important and to whom. These were very good people who worked very hard. Yet there were acute tensions over issues that had more to do with politics and control than health care itself. These political strains were hardly a surprise, but they affected the core values and beliefs of the organization's culture.

It was also obvious in staff sessions on patient- and family-centered care that there was a lot of concern about how little was being done to better engage patients and their families in their health-care decisions. For example, a mother who had brought her son into a doctor's office filed a complaint. She had been accompanied by a boyfriend, but the doctor discussed the child with him, ignoring the mother. She was furious. After all, the boyfriend had no role in the life of the child. How dare the doctor not address her?

The problem stemmed in part from the fact that the doctor was foreign-born and culturally inclined to address the man. But this was not an uncommon problem as doctors, nurses, and patients from different ethnic groups interacted in the health-care setting. And many physicians were pushing back on the idea that they had to change the way they interacted with patients.

When it came to pediatric demands, however, everyone was in agreement. For all of the physicians and the nurses—indeed, for the entire staff—the needs of children were of paramount importance. We watched as the staff embraced their roles as transformers, not just healers, for the children and their families in the region. Whether this was in the high-risk clinic, the neonatal intensive care unit, or in the local pediatricians' offices, it was easy to observe the different ways they expressed the importance of pediatric care.

The care that was available, however, was not enough. The community needed more access points and an expanded physician base. Some allergists had three-month-long waits for appointments. Other pediatricians were growing their practices faster than they could staff and support them. The community itself needed more wellness support; the center's medical residents served part of their training in local church venues, where they provided pediatric care.

We also conducted observational research among the patients, for whom the experience of going to a hospital is often as challenging as traveling in a foreign land. The patients' tension was evident as we saw them come through the front door and try to navigate their way through the halls. But we also noticed them re-enter the outside world in a new way as they left—perhaps with a new baby in their arms or with a cast on their leg—with hope for better days ahead. We watched patients coming and going and listened to their interactions with staff.

We spent time in the clinics and in various specialty centers, as well as in doctors' offices listening to patients discuss their needs and watching the physicians deal with them. As part of the process, we conducted some game-playing research with patients and their families to uncover how the experience at the center affected them. At one session, bariatric surgery patients repeatedly focused on how alone they felt when they were going through their surgery and recovery. That theme was expressed not only by the patients but also by their spouses. These kinds of concerns were confirmed by a nurse who had noticed a surgical patient in tears because he felt so alone. Physicians echoed this feeling; they felt their patients were uncomfortable coming to the center, where they felt lost and alone.

Culture Probes

We knew we needed to get a better understanding of the communities that the center was currently serving and those that it needed to expand into if it were to thrive. We began with interviews and storytelling sessions with leaders in the community. One recurring theme highlighted the importance of the medical center for the community and its vital role as a safety-net hospital. Each interviewee seemed to have a story to share about a child who had been injured riding a bike or cutting the grass or who contracted cancer, and the miraculous ways that the center's physicians had been able to heal them.

Yet, when I asked if they had ever gone to the hospital themselves, they typically said, "Oh, no. That's not my hospital or my doctor." The medical center was a great hospital—just not for anyone who was insured or who went to a doctor who didn't attend there.

When I interviewed the physicians, they and their staff were comfortable splitting their time between the medical center and one of the other hospitals. In fact, their office managers were very efficient at routing patients depending on their insurance status—insured went to the other city hospital, and the uninsured or those on Medicaid went to the medical center.

Farther away from the center of the city, we heard different stories. Some physicians in more distant areas occasionally sent patients to the center, according to their beliefs about the best place for care as well as their own ethnicity or racial background. But the city had a reputation as a dangerous place by this time, and this played a role in the physicians' decisions not to refer patients to the center, underscoring the fear factor and the sense of being alone there.

What Emerged from the Research?

As the center's interim senior vice president of branding, marketing, and physician services, I looked at the research we were amassing and identified areas to address. The medical center needed to

- build on the current familiarity and affection people had for the center;
- overcome the fear factor and the sense of being alone, regardless of where patients came from or who they were;
- leverage the new focus on the patient that was emerging in patient- and family-centered care;
- capitalize on the care with which staff—physicians, nurses, and other employees—treated the patients and their families when they were at the hospital and after they left; and
- demonstrate innovative approaches to delivering care that could separate and differentiate the center from the rest of the competitors in the local and regional market space.

In fact, we were able to implement a number of new programs that helped to rebrand the hospital, change the patient experience, and make the new center come alive to the local and regional communities. These programs also helped to start a culture change process.

Expanding Pediatrics

The importance of the center's role for children could not be underestimated. You didn't have to listen or watch for too long to see how it wrapped itself around its role as a pediatric center.

Children came into the emergency department for everything from fevers and asthma to injuries and accidents. Yet there was a shortage of care points and hours that working parents could take advantage of.

One of the ideas we tested was to set up a free, one-time day-and-evening clinic for back-to-school physicals for kids. The turnout was huge, and some parents not only brought in their own children but also their neighbors' and friends' kids. Clearly this was an unmet need, and while it did not continue as an annual event, it taught us a lot about how to deliver care in a more innovative way.

The other obvious need we discovered was for a children's hospital, and eventually the new and very successful children's medical center was launched.

You Are Never Alone

To counteract what was clearly a prevalent feeling of being alone at the center, we gathered the physician services team and identified one of the staff—let's call him Jamal—to start what we called the You Are Never Alone program. Jamal organized a team of volunteers who greeted and guided patients around the hospital, visited them at their bedside, and served as liaisons to keep their families informed.

The nurse manager who worked with bariatric surgery patients also realized the importance of making these patients feel like they had someone right there at their bedside; someone who could help them through the recovery phase as they changed their diets, altered their food consumption, and lost weight. Where the old process had been focused on the physician and attracting patients, it became clear that what was needed was a way to engage the patient and continue that relationship after the surgery.

New Opportunities in Men's Health

Through our research and a personal connection, we also uncovered a completely ignored market segment: men. We noticed that, by and large, men did not have primary care doctors, did not go to doctors regularly, and often did not continue to take prescribed medications. This crucial insight came about in part because one of the marketing team had an elderly father who had insurance but no physician. In fact, the staff member realized that his father had never really had a physician that he saw routinely. Like so many other men, the dad went to the emergency room when something was acutely wrong; he didn't feel he needed annual physicals or other services.

THROUGH OUR RESEARCH, WE UNCOVERED A COMPLETELY IGNORED MARKET SEGMENT.

This phenomenon plays out nationally, as we discovered. Only sixty-six percent of men have doctors, compared to ninety-two percent of women. In fact, women are three times more likely to see a doctor on a regular basis than men. Even though men on average die younger than women and have higher mortality rates for heart disease, cancer, stroke, and AIDS, trying to get a man to see a doctor is no easy task.

At the center, targeting men and focusing on men's health required some major changes in physician practices, hours of availability, and marketing messages. One of the physicians told us that his office was designed for women. From the colors in the waiting room to the process for examining a patient, he had really designed his office and trained his office staff to cater to his major patient community, women. Moreover, his hours made it difficult for a workingman to get an appointment. Men, the doctor said, were impostors when they sat on his examination table. If asked how he was, a male patient would say he was fine, though his wife or girlfriend would pipe up, "No, he's not." The perception among men was that they weren't supposed to be sick and that seeing a doctor, taking pills, and feeling weak was not manly.

In the summer of 2012, the center hosted its first Men's Health Summit, the result of the marketing team's extraordinary efforts to reach out and engage patients. It attracted more than one thousand men and their families, and the success that year prompted physicians to rethink how they served men in their communities.

As it turned out, the center was on the cusp of a larger movement underway at hospitals across the country, from Cleveland Clinic's Men's Health Clinic to New York University's Men's Health Center. While this was not something that it continued to pursue, the initial effort demonstrated the unmet needs of a market segment that was potentially an important patient base.

All these "brandable" initiatives served to make the center's experience tangible, focused, and differentiating. This wasn't just another medical center; it was clearly a place that wanted its patients to benefit from the care that it provided and delivered in ways that other medical centers could not.

That led to our rethinking the center's brand and the best way to communicate it to the market.

Building a Brand

As we shifted our focus from outside-in to inside-out, the marketing team and I began to develop a consistent branding strategy for both the internal staff and the external community. Within the center, the staff was delivering exceptional care in a unique way. How could we capture that and build an internal identity that reflected their efforts and celebrated them? Externally, the market needed a single-minded story that differentiated the medical center, honestly expressed what it offered, and answered the question "Why our medical center?"

We soon realized that we needed to leverage the deep bonds people in the region had with the children's hospital and the trauma center. The center had always been there for them when they needed exceptional care. At the same time, we had to sustain momentum in other service lines, such as cardiac surgery, bariatric surgery, and orthopedics.

The branding story we built was about the role of the medical center in keeping the community and each person within it healthy. The tagline was chosen, and we used advertising, billboards, events, and other communication methods to show how the center was working to make individuals and the community healthy. Yes, this medical center would be there when you needed it, but it could also help you stay safe and healthy outside of the hospital. While this was a little before the population health movement emerged, the powerfully consistent message differentiated our center from the other hospitals and demonstrated its important role in each person's life.

The next question was how best to relay that message to parents, kids, and the rest of the community. By now this was 2010, still fairly early in the evolution of social media and websites.

Nevertheless, we turned our attention to the center's

website, which was an archaeological ruin—basically a brochure that had no personality, did not capture the power of the brand, and was barely functional. It used no social media or blogs and was not connected to Facebook. We needed better ways to communicate to the outside world what was happening within the hospital, and we needed the community to engage with physicians, parents, patients, and family.

At the same time, consumers' behavior was beginning to change: People were judging products and services—including hospitals and physicians—before they experienced them. Patients were using search engines to find information about a hospital, a doctor, and a surgery, and even the price of that surgery. Today, we know that the online experience is the first and often the most critical contact point for consumers searching for a health-care need. Yet during those first years of transformation, this was a new idea.

The marketing team started by developing some award-winning advertising using patients' stories about their experiences and then turned to developing a website and social media strategy that helped those stories come alive. One of the staff understood that there was no better place than Facebook to start telling personal stories, particularly those that highlighted the medical center's focus on children. Together, we initiated social platforms and started having "conversations" with the community—for example, storytelling contests around Mother's and Father's Day, observations of important center milestones, and very special "alumni tales," in which community members recounted their special ties to the center dating from their births there.

These all allowed the community's deeply held affection for the center to shine through. Their Facebook community grew slowly at first; then it exploded as a place to celebrate patients and their families, new babies, birthdays, and survivor anniversaries. Even physicians had stories to share. Today, the center has thousands of Facebook likes and visitors. Its social media presence is exciting and reflects the energy of the institution. And it continuously outperforms other hospitals in raising community engagement.

The Right Culture for the Time

From the beginning, we were hired to help the center assess and change its culture. Working with a new human resource director, we had the Organizational Cultural Assessment Instrument (OCAI) and introduced a predominant university's culture change process to the center.

> AS IMPORTANT AS BRANDING IS, IT IS
> EQUALLY IMPORTANT THAT THE CULTURE
> IS IN SYNC WITH THAT MESSAGE.

As important as branding was for the patients and the medical community in articulating what the center was about, it was equally important that the hospital culture was in sync with that message. Inevitably that meant that certain aspects of the culture had to change—never an easy or comfortable process.

The OCAI, an online survey, enables an organization's staff to take a deep look at their culture and ask what it is and what they would prefer it to be in the future. Those were the questions the center was posing.

Almost sixty-five percent of the employees took the OCAI, and the results—hardly a surprise—were consistent throughout the hospital, even to the board of directors. They revealed a culture that was very top-down and hierarchical. We already knew that. For example, the CEO had to sign almost all of the checks, and most decision-making flowed up to managers or vice presidents, leaving those closest to the patients with little power. Remarkably, though, people at every level wanted that to change. The OCAI crystallized a desire for the culture to become more innovative, empowering, visionary, and collaborative.

Despite the consensus, the staff was not clear what becoming more collaborative really meant. Nor did they know how to empower employees and enable more innovation. Many employees had been at the medical center for years, some for their entire adult working lives. They might say the culture had to change, but they had little interest in changing themselves.

As a start, we took close to fifty managers and leaders to a local university's school of executive education for a week of training in culture change. It was both an opportunity to bond around the problem and to understand what had to happen. As the transition process began, however, both the president/CEO and the HR director left to accept positions elsewhere. It was beyond my scope to work on the culture change process. It was time for me to move on as well.

Nevertheless, the center had achieved a great deal. Despite a near-bankrupt local economy and anemic financials, the medical center was transformed from top to bottom, producing a seven-million-dollar surplus in just two years. By 2011, it had launched a children's hospital, constructed a thirty-million-dollar, state-of-the-art emergency and trauma center that cared for ninety thousand patients annually, built a new entrance and lobby, and initiated a program for patient- and family-centered care. Indeed, many in the community understood the center's value to the region and to them individually. The center had become "theirs."

Lessons Learned for Your Company

While you may or may not be a health-care organization, the medical center story is not that different from many organizations that are recovering from financial challenges and now dealing with new and often changing business markets. Typically, health-care organizations adapt to changing times by copying each other, benchmarking what they are doing against others who are respected and knowledgeable in the field. However, during health-care reform there are no benchmarks to follow. What about your organization? Here are four things you can learn from our experiences at the medical center.

1. You can make change fun.

    I don't mean that in a casual way. We know that the brain hates to change even when it knows it must. Play and games can help the brain see things in new ways so it can more readily accept change. People like to play and, when engaged in the process of change, they find that they are good at it. Similarly, the new world you are creating is like a new game. Once your people learn the rules and how to play their roles, they can be very good at it.

2. Do you have the right people on your team?

    This is always a key question that only you can answer. During changing times, the answer is not always clear. Employees' past performance may not be indicative of their future competency or ability to adapt to change in new business environments. I suggest getting into the trenches and seeing what your people are really doing. You'll be able to evaluate their capabilities by watching them and listening to their stories. As they talk to each other, you will learn a great deal about their true talents.

3. Tell your story often, in ways that resonate.

Too many companies are reluctant marketers. But if you don't tell your story, people will make one up for you. This was one of the key challenges at the medical center. Is it happening to you? In today's omni-channel world of story-telling, you have to tell your story often, use your current customers to help you tell it, and make it relevant to those you want as your customers (or patients, in the medical center's case). Don't forget that online storytelling must be managed carefully and daily.

4. Culture change might be needed.

Take the OCAI (www.ocai-online.com) yourself and see what it could do for you and your organization. Then have your entire company take it. See what bubbles up about how they see the culture today and how they would prefer it to be in the future. You might be ready, and you might really need to shift the way you are doing things, as well as the values, beliefs, and symbols that hold your organization together—your culture.

CHAPTER 6

....

A PREMIUM PLUMBING MANUFACTURER

WHAT HAPPENS WHEN you have a great new product, one that you know is the best in terms of innovation but that isn't selling well? Your sales team insists that customers don't see its benefits. Or that it isn't required by building codes. Or perhaps that your "good customers" simply cannot justify the hefty expense of investing in it. It may be a terrific product, but clearly there's a real problem with it that's hard to see.

That was exactly the challenge facing a top-of-the-line plumbing manufacturer a few years back. This successful manufacturer of water fountains, sinks, faucets, and kitchen cabinetry had created a hydration station for refillable water bottles as a line extension for its popular water fountains. The new product took off well, but it quickly became obvious that selling hydration stations to buyers was going to require a different approach. Simply relying on the company's traditional distribution channels was not working yet.

To help them drive growth, the company brought on a new president and a vice president of finance—both of whom attended one of my "Change Matters" workshops. Afterward, the three of us began to talk about why the new product wasn't selling well. Could I help them figure out what to do about that?

We worked with the company and as it turned out, the hydration station would indeed eventually open up an entirely new market for them, but none of us knew that at the beginning.

Our client was known for its values and traditions, and over time, it expanded the sales of its wares into big-box, home-improvement retailers and to commercial and residential builders.

Water fountains were often required by building codes to be installed in new construction, and the company had captured a prominent position in the water fountain industry in the United States. It had experienced major growth early on and with new home construction booming, it looked like the company was positioned for more of the same going forward.

However, construction soon slowed, and by 2008 the residential real estate market had crashed. The subsequent steep decline in new home construction severely affected the company's plumbing supply and kitchen cabinet business. In addition—and significantly—there was very little commercial construction at the time, which adversely affected water fountain sales. The company's executives were facing a down market that was going to require some serious innovations and exceptional business management skills to overcome.

Luckily, the president had been recruited to infuse the business with new processes, more effective systems, and a more competitive advantage. In his variety of previous leadership roles, his sales results had been exceptional. He really understood how to change a company, and the company felt strongly that they had the right man for the times.

In a way, he was fortunate to be forced to deal with the recession, since it gave everyone in the company a common crisis to respond to. The massive crash hurt the company's business across the board. However, it also provided a tremendous opportunity for the president to redesign not only what the company did—but how it did it.

He started the push to turn the company around by issuing a challenge to each and every employee. He wanted the employees to begin looking at ways to make the company stronger, better, and more efficient in the work that they did.

He knew it was more than just a matter of how many factories or people the company had. All the procedures, processes, and methods they had used were going to be reevaluated. He believed that change was not going to happen from above. Consequently, the company began to examine everything they did in a very systematic way.

To begin, the president got the staff to examine their business in new ways, searching for commonalities in order to build better consistency and reduce duplication. He also realized that the company had been so focused on growth that it was ignoring what the customers needed and wanted. The company gave customers what *they* thought they needed. But as management began to analyze their business and their customers more closely, they realized their own processes were not necessarily designed for either the customer's benefit or for the company's profits.

To redesign the entire financial and analytical business management systems, the company's new advisors knew from the get-go that they couldn't afford to settle for a few minor upgrades. Instead, a total renovation was launched that included profitability analytics, customer relationship management, a rolling forecast, and a balanced scorecard. What the company began to understand was that many of its basic operating assumptions had to change. Customers weren't all profitable customers. Systems weren't uniformly effective in producing exceptional products at profitable margins. And without a shared system, teams across the organization often worked at odds with each other.

This cultural transformation set an exceptional stage for the work to be done for the innovative but underperforming hydration station.

The Product That Wasn't Selling

The notion of a hydration station for refillable water bottles had gotten its start when employees began noticing that when people went through airport security with empty water bottles, they then had to twist and turn them in order to fill them at traditional water fountains. To fill this gap, the R&D team was asked to create a prototype hydration station with water flow that would be sufficient, filtered, and easy to use. Wisely, they focused on the technical hurdles: It was often hard to position an empty water bottle and fill it at a water fountain, and filling a bottle took a long time.

The leadership team thought that filling a sixteen-ounce bottle should take less than ten seconds, something that at least one engineer said was impossible. (Traditional fountains take at least twenty seconds.) That is when another engineer took on the challenge. He and his colleagues devised a way to push the water through the filter—a block of carbon encased in plastic—more quickly. The result was the company's new innovation. Three times the size of a standard drinking fountain, the new filter could dispense sixteen ounces in about five seconds if the water delivered was at room temperature, seven seconds if it had to be chilled.

To tackle consumers' fears of germs, the company's engineers figured out how people could fill their water bottles without having to touch the fountain. Their solution: When a bottle was placed under the spigot, an infrared sensor automatically turned on the flow.

To sell the new product, the company had turned to its traditional distribution channels—manufacturers' representatives selling to architects and engineers, building owners, and facility managers—and the existing market, but soon it became painfully clear that the "traditional" method wasn't working. Distributors weren't sure what they were selling, and buyers weren't interested in spending additional money on hydration stations. Filling bottles was not a big concern for them and certainly not required by building codes.

For the company, the big question was what real benefit did a hydration station offer? It wasn't required by code or ordinances. Was an easier way to refill a water bottle a compelling reason for a facilities manager to purchase one? What was the company missing?

First Things First: Lay the Groundwork

Once we were brought into the picture, we decided to approach this problem in three ways, all built around the fact that we didn't really know why someone would want to buy a hydration station, much less buy the company's innovative one.

First, I did some research on the water fountain, observed how people used it, and then found out what the literature said about why the water fountain was required in US building codes. Second, we set up a two-day retreat for the company's senior leadership, so that we could take them through our process of discovery. Third, we were asked to conduct an identical retreat with some of their key people to see what they could come up with.

Fortunately, it happened to be an opportune time to revitalize the drinking fountain. Year by year, Americans were drinking more water and fewer high-calorie soft drinks. By 2012, tap and bottled water accounted for thirty percent of the typical

American's liquid intake, up from sixteen percent two decades before, according to the Beverage Marketing Corporation. Nearly half of that water came from taps, including drinking fountains.

The origin of drinking fountains reflected the public's need for clean, cost-free drinking water. Back in the mid-nineteenth century in London, water provided by private companies was generally inadequate for the rapidly growing population, and the water was often contaminated. As a result, legislation made water filtration compulsory and moved water intakes on the River Thames above the sewage outlets. A movement to promote public drinking fountains followed, and soon an estimated seven thousand people a day were using them.

In the United States, in 1889, the then-small Kohler Water Works (now Kohler Company) in Wisconsin added drinking fountains to the faucets it already produced. And in 1896, a young man named Halsey W. Taylor lost his father to typhoid fever caused by a contaminated water supply. The would-be entrepreneur then dedicated his life to providing a safe, sanitary drink of water in public places. He founded the company that bears his name in 1912, and in 1926, he perfected and patented what is now known as the Double Bubbler, which projects two separate streams of water which converge to provide a fuller and more satisfying drink.

All of these inventions and innovations have nicely dovetailed with today's recent discussions about public water fountains. In 2012, the EPA began collaborating with US mayors "to reinvigorate our nation's supply of public drinking fountains" and "publicize the benefits of drinking safe, affordable tap water." According to the agency's "Bring Back the Water Fountain!" web page, promoting the public fountain is one way to foster an understanding of the tremendous efforts of approximately 155,000 public water systems in cities and municipalities throughout the United States. These public systems treat, filter, and deliver tap water to homes, businesses, and institutions 24 hours a day, 365 days a year, at an average cost of $0.002 per gallon—significantly less than the cost of a bottle of water, without any of the landfill issues.

Indeed, demand for clean, safe water has been on the upswing everywhere you look in America, and around the world, but the real growth for our client came from an entirely unexpected source and through a chance discovery while we were working with their management on finding their new market space.

What Needed Figuring Out: People's Relationships with Drinking Fountains

We began our research by hanging out in public places to see what the water fountain experience was like for people when they refilled their water bottles *and* when they bought new bottles of water. Unexpectedly, some people told us that they still considered drinking fountains unsanitary and even dangerous. Parents spoke about their concern for their children, who, when they leaned over to take a drink, had been shoved by bullies and ended up with broken teeth. There is extensive research on how people feel about water fountains and why they are often reluctant to use them[1].

To gather "on the ground" information firsthand, I stood next to people in airports and watched how they used water fountains there. One man in the Chicago airport had a bottle he was trying to fill; by awkwardly tipping it sideways, he got it "sort of filled." It was functional, but neither easy nor fun—an important piece of the puzzle that I filed away.

As a parallel, equally important endeavor, we researched

the movement to eliminate plastic in landfills and found that disposable water bottles were playing an important role in that volatile and highly emotional arena. On many college campuses, in hospitals, and within organizations with strong sustainability movements, sales of plastic bottles were being eliminated. Hydration stations in cafeterias were emerging, although slowly. We observed some of these and watched how people filled their cups or bottles there.

What fascinated me was the disconnection between the need and the solution. Here was free water, widely available through a fountain that people were uncomfortable using. Plastic bottles were simpler and easier to transport. Refillable bottles were somewhat challenging but could be filled in any number of ways, either at water fountains or at sinks. So, I asked myself, what was the value of a hydration station?

Shifting from Problem to Solution

To further get at the heart of the problem—and the solution— we held a two-day retreat with our client's senior leaders to deconstruct their current strategy and see what they might be missing. Clearly, they had done a great deal of research. They knew they needed a new way to sell the product and create demand, and our retreat workshops were designed to help that process move forward.

Interestingly, what was revealed in our management workshops was that the problem lay in the sales process, the inability of distributors to sell something that wasn't required by code, and the resistance of buyers to spend money on a hydration station. The discussion centered on how to overcome these objections.

Some of the ideas that emerged from the retreat were good ones. Turns out, the company had entered a market that already had two hydration station competitors. The big difference was that our client's product management team had conducted research to make sure the right features were added to their unit so that it could successfully compete in this new market. The client's design was built around having a hands-free operation, fast-fill filtration, antimicrobial features, and a bottle counter. Far better than other models entering the market, their superior features seemed enough to warrant sales.

However, when we conducted a similar workshop with middle management, R&D developers, marketing leaders, distributors, and manufacturers, different ideas emerged. As we have seen time and time again, quite often transformative ideas come from individuals who are not running a business unit or driving the sales force. Outsiders beyond the core management team can often uncover things that others are discounting.

This is exactly what happened with our client's team. On the second day of the workshop for mid-level managers, we zeroed in on who could really use their hydration station. Who were the nonusers with unmet needs?

As it happened, there *was* a standout client. The highest visibility for the company's hydration station had come from the introduction of the units at a college. Yet the college was not a typical customer.

The college had bought the units to begin a major program of eliminating the sale of plastic water bottles on campus. The idea had actually emerged two years earlier in one of the college's courses. At first, students wanted to ban plastic water bottles altogether. But the threat of eliminating a popular product from campus aroused considerable resistance.

A science student who was active in an on-campus environmental group remembered that some students were upset, because they wanted to keep their bottled water.

The environmental group stressed the advantages of eliminating bottles. But the student government was still not completely sold on the idea. They held blind tests, challenging students to taste the difference between tap water and bottled water. Few could. The group also emphasized that most plastic bottles are not recycled and that it is highly wasteful (and damaging to the environment) to use oil and additional water to package a product that can be obtained for free.

By the end of 2009, the activists had convinced enough of their peers to persuade the student government to change the college's policy. The college installed the hydration stations in 2010, and each incoming freshman got a stainless steel water bottle to use and refill.

Then the college ran a campus-wide campaign to get students to refill those water bottles, which made great strides in reducing sales of the plastic containers. The once-controversial change became part of the routine. Bottled water sales dropped ninety percent after the new policies were initiated on campus. The movement was so successful that it got national news coverage about the college's efforts to eliminate sales of the plastic water bottle.

To top it all off, the filling station won an award for innovation. Yet there was still no line out the door to buy it. Where, then, was the gap?

Was the Future Right in Front of Them? Yes!

In one of the middle-management workshops our client held, one manager said something, almost casually, that framed the entire problem in a completely new way. What he recognized was *the value to the college* of those hydration stations, which were providing the college with the opportunity to reduce—almost eliminate—sales of plastic water bottles. What did that mean for the market space that our client was looking to penetrate?

Specifically, did customers actually want something that could help them fill their water bottles and, in the process, eliminate the virtually unending pileup of plastic water bottles? Perhaps, then, the focus should be on sustainability directors, facilities managers, and others who were concerned with reducing the size of landfills. Was there a different way to see the market potential and, in so doing, open up that market in new, innovative ways?

The facilities manager at the college had certainly been the one to latch on to the hydration stations as a must-have addition to the campus. But it was the sustainability directors who had been searching for a solution to water bottle filling, something that went beyond ease of use. They were looking at the far bigger picture: shifting student behavior away from endlessly purchasing plastic water bottles and, instead, refilling bottles they already owned. This would fulfill the college's student-driven mission of reducing items going to landfills and increasing the college's commitment to environmental sustainability. (In the United States at that time, some fifteen hundred plastic water bottles were purchased every second. This was a major environmental concern, even if they could be recycled.)

Almost without meaning to, our client's strategy became meeting the needs of multiple customers by offering an alternative to bottled water. The key was getting to those customers, defining their needs, and explaining how the company's product could solve their problem. Every customer had a different requirement, and the company's product had the right features to meet their needs.

What came out of the company's retreats was the lesson to not focus on what the competition was doing but to create their own path for their products. Their hydration station could not only help sustainability directors fulfill their mission but could also help others who could see the ease and speed with which bottles could be refilled as the units were installed in major cities; in airports, in locations visible just beyond the security gates; and in K–12 schools and colleges.

As we presented these breakthrough realizations to senior management, we could see how the ideas were confirming some of their own earlier assumptions and research results. Having already been in the process of developing the strategy, the management team saw how the hydration stations had tremendous potential among eco-friendly nonusers—potential customers whom management hadn't focused on before. The company now recognized that it would need a number of innovative solutions to occupy that market, create demand, and make it simpler and easier for students, employees, managers, and others to use and buy their hydration stations.

To capture this new water-bottle-filling market space before anyone else did, the company hired new salespeople and focused their attention on sustainability directors at corporations and academic institutions across the United States. The marketing department revised the company's website and expanded its e-commerce capabilities. They developed a marketing campaign promoting hydration stations to university campuses and created tools to focus concurrently on multiple customers in the sales process.

Ultimately, sales of the hydration station began to grow rapidly. College students across the country contacted the company to see how they could bring filler stations onto their campuses—some individuals even clamored to buy them for their own use.

As our assignment concluded and the leadership team

reflected on our work with them, we were told that it was not what we did, but how we helped them see things in new ways.

Lessons Learned for Your Company

As you know by now, we have worked with many companies that were facing their acres of diamonds but couldn't see them. Here's hoping that you can use anthropology and these stories to help you see yours. If you are ready to try, here are four things about our experience that might work for you and your company.

1. Old business processes may be just that—old.

    The fact that you and your distribution channels are comfortable selling your products as you always have, to buyers who always bought, doesn't mean a thing as you look to the future. This is a good time to rethink how you are distributing your products and leveraging today's new channels (the Internet, Amazon, direct-to-end-user or direct-to-consumer). You don't need to scrap the old. But this just might be a good time to expand it, reflect on it, test options, and keep testing. Make sure you have the data and can hear what it is telling you, so you can adjust and adapt as the channels change.

2. Acres of diamonds are all around you.

    Our client's acres were right in front of them, but they could not see them. Are you like that? Try bringing your team together in a think session and take apart what you are doing today as you look for opportunities that you are maybe currently discounting. Then take a look at those discounted opportunities and see how to turn them into viable, even great, ones. Or go hang out and see what is happening out there in the field. In so doing, you might just come across your diamonds waiting for someone (you!) to craft a better solution.

3. New leaders see things in new ways.

I am not going to suggest that you need to replace yourself if you are the president or CEO. I'm simply saying that maybe you need new eyes. Give it some thought. Perhaps a consultant might unleash some fresh ideas. What you're seeking is that balance between stability and innovation that helps you adapt to changing business environments quickly and effectively.

4. Don't stop seeing with new eyes.

Once you have had an aha! moment, your brain will start to see things in new ways. Don't stop it! It is far easier to revert back to what you always thought before than to keep going in the new, unfamiliar direction. Don't go backward with old eyes; boldly go forward with new ones. It is work for your brain but will pay off in "diamonds."

---

1   http://www.ncbi.nlm.nih.gov/pmc/articles/PMC3134515/

....

CHAPTER 7

BENJAMIN OBDYKE

WE HAD A call one morning in 2011 from Pennsylvania. The man on the other end of the line, Michael Coulton, was now the general manager of a family firm, Benjamin Obdyke, which had turned over its future to him. The challenge? The company had been around as a major innovator in roofing and siding products for 150 years. They had some patented roofing products that were coming off patent, and generics were already challenging the company's hold on the roofing market. They had other excellent wall products too, but the crash in new home construction that had started in 2006 and been exacerbated by the recession of 2008 was killing their business. Sales and margins had shrunk. Could I help?

I had been referred to Coulton by the chair of one of the Vistage International CEO groups where I give workshops and speeches each year. I didn't know much about Benjamin Obdyke or its industry, but I didn't have to. What was evident to me was that the current plan—more of the same and hope for a recovery—was probably not going to help the firm climb back even when the housing industry restarted. Benjamin Obdyke had some very large competitors on both the roofing and siding sides, such as GAF, Owens Corning, Certainteed, DuPont, and Dow. New or renewed growth was going to require not just a good product or even a superb one. The company was going to need new markets and a strategy to tackle them.

Coulton was aware of that. He and Dave Campbell, president and CEO of Obdyke, had read *Blue Ocean Strategy* and wanted to embrace those ideas. Blue Ocean Strategy® is a concept, method, and tool kit developed by Renée Mauborgne and W. Chan Kim in their book by that name, which describes the pair's research involving 150 US companies in fifty industries. What they found was that successful companies adapted to changing times by reconstructing the market space, creating demand (not just responding to it), and devising value innovation (not just adding value in an existing industry solution).

I became a Blue Ocean Strategist because the concepts were built around a very anthropological model. One of the core elements of seeking a Blue Ocean is to go visually exploring and to keep testing concepts in very experiential ways. For a company, that means that rather than embrace a traditional strategy of crafting a competitive position in a market that already exists and capturing market share away from other companies, that it embrace the Blue Ocean approach, which consists of creating uncontested market space, making the competition irrelevant, creating new demand, and keeping costs low while differentiating itself from competitors.

Coulton and Campbell had gone to a Blue Ocean training program in Erie, Pennsylvania. They had three days of great training, but they were left with a lot of questions. What were they supposed to look for? How would they recognize a potentially big idea for redesigning their traditional strategy? Were they to remain innovative product designers and manufacturers? Or were they supposed to create a new market space? For which nonusers and why? And what was "visual exploring"?

As Coulton told it at the training program, "We went 'exploring' by going out to a Barnes & Noble, a smaller bookstore, and then to a library to observe the differences and look for ideas, unmet needs, and ways to craft a new strategy. But we didn't really come back with a skill set to let us apply Blue Ocean thinking to Obdyke. We needed a hand, which was when we reached out to you."

I began by visiting Obdyke and meeting Coulton, who turned out to be a thoughtful young man from Pennsylvania who intuitively understood the business he was taking over and how he needed to change it. Tall, fit, and full of energy, he seemed like a teammate who was ready to roll up his sleeves to craft a game plan.

He was a two-decade veteran of the building-products industry and had spent his entire career at Obdyke, focused for the most part on developing innovative products that met the needs of builders and professional contractors. As president of the Building Enclosure Moisture Management Institute, Coulton was well respected in the industry and held, alone or with others, eleven US and Canadian patents. Marketing and strategy development were relatively new for him, though the company itself had a terrific history of invention and adaptation.

The firm had been founded in 1868 by one Benjamin P. Obdyke, who invented and patented the round corrugated downspout, beginning a long tradition of manufacturing innovative, quality building products. Obdyke employees have always been proud of the company's commitment to new product designs that help architects, builders, and contractors "Build Better." But it wasn't clear how to leverage that culture going forward.

Over the years, the company and product line had grown to include a variety of rain-carrying equipment, roof edging, and trims, while the manufacturing process included roll formers and various stamping dies.

In 1988, Obdyke acquired the patent for the first rolled ridge vent, which they marketed as Roll Vent. This inaugurated a new era of other innovative products, such as Rapid Ridge; Cedar Breather, the first wood-roofing ventilating underlayment; Home Slicker, the first rolled product to provide drainage and air flow in rain-screen wall assemblies; and eventually HydroGap, a house wrap with unique spacers attached to provide drainage within wall assemblies.

By 1997, the company was operating twenty-six roll formers in a 200,000-square-foot manufacturing and distribution facility in Warminster, Pennsylvania, when it was approached by another well-established Pennsylvania gutter manufacturer. Berger Brothers was interested in acquiring the metal manufacturing portion of the business. Based on the growth of their newer products, Obdyke decided to sell that portion of the business.

The sale called for some new approaches to strategy and their identity. Obdyke had always manufactured its own products. Now someone else would do that? So what role would the company play in the supply chain? It wasn't a distributor. And it was loyal to its distribution channels, so it wasn't going to compete with them either. Instead, management realized that the firm's role was twofold: invent better products to help builders build better, and learn how to become exceptional marketers to architects, engineers, builders, and contractors who would then demand Obdyke products.

All that was history. In 2011, there were other opportunities to be exploited; it was just a matter of identifying them.

> ULTIMATELY, WE WERE LOOKING FOR GAPS,
> STORIES THAT CUSTOMERS AND WOULD-BE
> CUSTOMERS WERE TALKING ABOUT, TRENDS
> THEY WERE THINKING ABOUT, PAIN POINTS
> THEY COULDN'T EASILY RESOLVE.

I began with a process to help the team do several things that were central to applying both anthropological and Blue Ocean theory and methods to the business. Ultimately, we were looking for gaps, stories that customers and would-be customers were talking about, trends they were thinking about, pain points they couldn't easily resolve. I was curious to see what the team couldn't see. But unless Coulton and his managers came to see and understand the opportunities as well, my analysis would be useless. They had to be part of the discovery process or we ran the risk of having consultant fatigue—a situation where they let me do the exploring and then discounted my observations. Not a very good approach to rebuilding the business.

So what specifically did we do?

First, we took the team out of the office for two days of discovery. Our goal was to build an idea bank of possibilities and set a plan for further exploration.

Two things emerged from that retreat: ideas and the realization that the team was less than excited about changing the business. The tensions we saw percolate up were not unexpected. Some of the folks were relatively new to the organization and very engaged, even excited about the possibilities of where the company could go. Others were cautious. They wanted to see what came out of the two days together. And then there was the old guard who had been in the business a long time and were skeptical of a consultant suggesting they should change.

They were hoping that I would go away. They *knew what they knew* really well and had to be convinced there were truly "blue oceans" that Obdyke could find and exploit.

Nonetheless, the process of change began. There was an abundance of ideas, some that involved incremental changes or value creation, others that could open new markets or capitalize on those that they were ignoring.

For example, there were geographic markets—such as the South or Southwest—in which they were not selling any of their HydroGap or other moisture management products. As far as anyone at Obdyke knew, no one in those areas needed moisture-protection technology under their shingles or wall finishes. But was it possible that maybe they did?

Another question was why they had refused to sell to big-box stores such as Lowe's, Menards, and The Home Depot. Their reasoning was that they had always protected their traditional distributors. That was the same reason they hadn't sold products online or through Amazon. Yet online sales, even to contractors in the business-to-business world, were growing rapidly.

There were also interesting ideas about how to use the technology for new applications. They had inquiries from Canada about how to keep campsite beds moisture-free. And a company in Massachusetts had been using the material to absorb water in homes that had experienced flooding or bathroom malfunctions. All these ideas were promising.

The next step was to spend some time with the staff, listening to phone calls and looking at emails. So much information comes through touch points like these, where users or consumers of the product interact with staff, that it can be a tremendous source of ideas, recognition of unmet needs, and insights into how the company is viewed by others. Our job is to begin to see and connect those dots of possibilities that are all too often overlooked or discounted by employees who just want to deal with the customer and move on to solving the next problem.

What did we find? In the phone calls and particularly in the emails, there were questions from people who wanted Obdyke's products but couldn't find them nearby. At that point the company really did not have any e-commerce capabilities. It sold its products through distributors and protected their "clients"—those distributors—by not competing with them through its own online distribution channel. Further, distribution was by and large in the Northeast and Midwest. The reason—historical pattern, chance, or design—was immaterial.

As we analyzed the inbound requests, we discovered that there were people across the United States, particularly in the Southwest and West, who were searching for Obdyke products online and then emailing or calling to find out where they could buy them locally. For many, that wasn't possible. While this was an irritating problem from the customer's perspective, it was also perplexing to us. Why was the distribution channel so limited and sacred? Why didn't Obdyke think that people in other parts of the country might need their building products? What else was the company discounting, overlooking, ignoring, or denying?

The email analysis led us to hold idea sessions with the Obdyke team to go over what people were telling us and what was *not* being done to respond. These were very creative people. I was simply facilitating a process that took them beyond what they were doing in the current business into thinking about the future.

Then we explored further. Since the distributors were considered sacred customers, we suggested going out with some of Obdyke's sales team to find out how the distributors were adapting to the construction slowdown. Not surprisingly, they told us they were cutting inventory and limiting selections.

Some of the distributors, mostly small family-owned lumberyards that served local markets, clearly maintained a wait-and-hope strategy. Since they were the primary distribution channels for Obdyke's roofing products and wraps, it was difficult to hear that they weren't ordering as much product for stock as they used to. They might put it in their catalogue and have it available if someone came in and wanted it, but they weren't going to invest in it for inventory purposes unless there was more demand.

At a meeting with the owner of a multisite distributor of lumber supplies, we listened for an hour to *his* strategy of managing in a slow economy, which basically consisted of trying to steal other distributors' customers.

Nonetheless, two ideas emerged from that conversation. First, it was clear that Obdyke was a valuable resource at education events for contractors and a leader in contractor education generally. This was a role that Obdyke had played over the years, and the distributor appreciated (and capitalized on) Obdyke's commitment to improving building materials and processes and sharing ideas and new products with the industry. How to leverage this was not yet clear, but the value the firm played in educating the market was not one I had anticipated.

It was the second insight that was really important, however. I had asked the distributor about where he saw growth in the industry. Where was there action in the market? His answer was stucco, particularly stucco remediation. Many Pennsylvania residents had stucco covering their homes and town houses. Moisture easily got between the stucco and the wood beneath it, and that was creating mold and rot. For the lumber business, this had generated a lot of demand for new windows, flashing, and masonry.

As we walked out of the meeting, I had a question for Dave Campbell and Obdyke's sales manager: Couldn't your products work for stucco remediation? What about HydroGap, the high-end house wrap with its unique moisture-removal technology?

Their first reaction was, "Well, we don't sell to the masonry market." When I asked why not, the answer was, "Well we don't." It took only a minute more, however, before the sales manager added, "But we can, and we should." And Campbell chimed in, "And we should do it fast."

This was a real unmet need among nonusers of Obdyke's products, but it didn't have to be. Many of their former contractors were now working in the remediation business. They constituted a huge market opportunity but one that had been totally ignored. Why not market to them? But how?

We came back to Obdyke filled with ideas and enthusiasm and eventually did three things.

First, one of the questions that had come out of our original workshop was why wasn't Obdkye selling in the South or Southwest? Or even in the Far West? The initial explanation was that there was less need for the products in those geographic regions.

However, when I reviewed where their phone calls and email inquiries were coming from, they turned out to be from the very part of the United States that "didn't need them." Digging deeper, and following up with actual interviews, we realized that the inquiries were not just for new home construction but also for restoring those stucco homes that had water damage and mold.

It didn't take long for the discussion to turn from "we don't sell in those areas" to "*how* can we sell in those areas?" With the Internet generating interested and qualified leads in areas where Obdyke didn't have distributors, it became far easier for the company to become a distributor itself. There was no risk and great upside potential to making products available through a direct-shipping model where it could convert inquiries into sales where there was no distributor.

This also meant that Obdyke needed a different e-commerce website that facilitated these transactions, as well as a strategy for reassuring current distributors that it wasn't trying to compete with them.

Second, we looked at Obdyke's distributors, mostly mid-market and smaller family-owned lumberyards in the Northeast and Midwest. The company had never tried to place its products in large big-box stores, like Lowe's, The Home Depot, or Menards, even though Menards claimed to be the largest retailer of home shingling, which was exactly the market that Obdyke served.

Obdyke had a great sales team. Yet, concerned about competing with their existing distributors, the salespeople were reluctant to call on Menards and see how they could gain distribution through those stores. Instead, using "research" as an excuse, I was the one who called on Menards, which turned out to be very interested in carrying the products—of course, at the right price.

Third, we wanted to take a close look at Obdyke's brand positioning. Was the company simply about roofing and siding products, or did it offer something unique, something that homeowners renovating their houses or homebuilders seeking high-end solutions would go out of their way to get? To find out, we accompanied the Obdyke team to a major trade show in Las Vegas.

There, the Obdyke folks set up their booth outside of the building in a space set aside for innovative home builders and building products that were positioned as leading edge. As I surveyed the other vendors at the show, it became clear that Obdyke really did occupy a space that set it apart from the rest. Its products were unique and presented in a way that communicated that difference. Whether they were aware of it or not, the Obdyke employees were living a brand built on innovation and a willingness to help others "Build Better"—a culture that stretched back to the original founder's enterprise after the Civil War.

What emerged from all this were several more ideation sessions where we pushed the model in new directions. We explored questions like these:

- Why are we so reluctant to look outside of our traditional distribution channel? Are there other ways of getting products in the hands of those who want them?

- What is happening in e-commerce that we aren't paying attention to? Coulton asked if people, especially building professionals, were really buying construction products online. When we did a search, we found that Amazon was expanding rapidly into the business-to-business arena. In fact, all of Obdyke's products were being sold by their distributors and others online, often at higher prices.

- Why aren't we selling through the big-box stores like Lowe's, Menards, and The Home Depot? Could we open up that market without jeopardizing our current distributors?

- What did people in the South and West need with our house-wrap products? There is a lot of stucco there. Maybe they need our house wraps the same way the stucco remediation market does in the Northeast.

- Could we service inquiries ourselves in parts of the country where we don't have distributors? What are contractors doing that we could leverage?

- What about emails and calls from one-off customers? AAA Flood, for example, was using Home Slicker to help absorb water in flooded homes. Who else could use these products in new ways?

All this was consistent with the company's core brand and culture. Suddenly everyone could begin to see the possibilities of creating incremental value.

For the large market that was in full swing around stucco remediation, they had to find ways to penetrate it; they couldn't be just another product for contractors who were doing that work.

As background research, Coulton even had a contractor come to his home to do an assessment of the stucco covering. What he learned helped him realize that many in the industry were basically putting new stucco up over what had been there before, without a wrap to drain the moisture. In all probability this would lead to more mold and rot in the near future.

With his concern for educating the contractor and the industry—not just selling them products—and recognizing that trying to only go through the traditional distributor system was a challenge, he had his team create an entirely new approach built around teaching the contractor and the consumer how to build better.

Obdyke created a new website focused on this approach and designed it to help consumers know what to ask a contractor and how to use Obdyke products in their stucco restoration. It was also designed to help contractors more easily get the right products to remediate the problems. If stucco was creating mold and rotting the wood, wouldn't a house wrap that pulled the water away—HydroGap, for example—transform how they did their work?

Similarly, to address the access and distribution challenges, their main website also became an e-commerce site. First the company used another online distribution channel, but it didn't take too long for Obdyke to realize that it could do even better on its own.

Going Forward

How is Obdyke doing today?

Coulton says that there is really "exciting stuff here—online sales grew five times in 2014. We are launching a new initiative into services for building professionals. And we reorganized into two business units—one for Ridge Ventilation focused on a push strategy, utilizing distribution, and one for building better products and services, focused on creating awareness, conversion, and ways of getting products in the hands of builders and contractors the way they want to source them."

Their products now include stucco-appropriate house wraps branded and marketed to that new market. And the new stucco remediation website goes beyond the contractor to the consumer who needs a stucco home remediated but doesn't really know how to build better. Most importantly, Obdyke's distribution channels have expanded, and the company sells its products everywhere.

Coulton was expecting online sales to grow geometrically in 2015. What has been particularly interesting to him is that users and nonusers of his products, services, and solutions have a lot of different ways of engaging with the company. No longer do you need to be just one thing distributed in just one way, he now realizes. One recent buyer was told he could get his order shipped to him after an online purchase or he could pick it up at a local distributor. (Obdyke still likes to provide the choice where it can.) "Nope," the contractor said, "I would rather get it online and ship it directly to my customer's building site."

It turns out that one of the things that Obdyke continues to build better is the company itself.

Lessons Learned from Benjamin Obdyke for Your Company

I always like to share the Benjamin Obdyke story, because it is full of ideas that can help other companies avoid a "stall out" when their business slumps. Here are four ideas that could be of help to you and your organization.

> WANT TO CHANGE? HAVE A
> CRISIS OR CREATE ONE.

1. Want to change? Have a crisis or create one.
   This is never something I wish for anyone. Yet, pushing a company into new markets, transforming a business model, and creating a new corporate culture all require some heavy lifting. If it is time for your company to change, it might also be time to create some drama. A crisis forces people out of their comfort zone into new territory where they must change to survive. If you are not ready to have a crisis, think about how to create the same energy and focus that a crisis causes and use these to reinvent your organization.

2. Lunch and listen with a client.

I'm assuming you like to go out with clients, entertain them, and try to sell them "one more thing." Instead, try taking them out for a lunch and listen. Invite along someone else from your organization if you don't want to do this all alone. Then ask the client to tell you about the trends in his or her own industry, the challenges they are facing, and some of the ways they are trying to adapt to new times or business pain points. Don't sell them anything. Just let them tell you stories, encourage them to share more, and listen carefully for things they're coping with that could turn into big ideas for your own company. Stucco as an emerging market for Obdyke came from a listening session. What could come from yours?

3. Are you ready to expand your marketing capabilities?

Far too many of our clients and mid-market CEOs whom we speak with are struggling to grow, yet have limited marketing expertise or resources. Sadly, this means that they are missing out on their key business strategy for growth—great marketing. With the growth of inbound or digital marketing, the investment is very manageable and the dashboards can quickly tell you what is working and what is not. Obdyke discovered how to "Build Better Online," targeting both consumers and contractors. You might find it of great value as well.

4. New geographies might offer new opportunities.

When we analyzed Obdyke's emails and discovered they were coming from all over the country—where they didn't sell their products—we were startled. The assumption that their products weren't needed in the warmer climates was based on perceptions, not realities. Are you doing something similar? Where are your growth markets, really? Maybe in areas where you don't think your product is needed or where you don't have distribution because of perceptions unfounded in fact? Take a look at your emails and see what you could learn.

....

CHAPTER 8

PARAGONRX

I ALWAYS LIKE to work with young, emerging companies, and ParagonRx was no exception. It was 2008. As a result of a presentation, I met Jeffrey Fetterman and Gary Slatko, who had founded ParagonRx in Delaware seven years earlier to define better ways to prescribe and appropriately use certain complex medications.

The men were a great team. Fetterman, in his late forties at the time, had a background in nuclear safety, and marketing and product development in the pharmaceutical industry, and was co-founder and president of ParagonRx. He was the entrepreneur, very innovative and open to new ideas. He had that uncanny ability to see possibilities and apply methodologies from one industry setting to another. He didn't mind working in a vacuum, where rules weren't clearly laid out. Truly a visionary, he could see what was coming in the world of health risk and imagine how to help his pharmaceutical company clients mitigate those risks. They just needed his vision, his methods, and his tool kits.

Slatko, the company's fifty-year-old medical director, was a physician with a long, successful professional career in the drug safety arena. He led the firm's pharmaceutical safety and risk-management consulting practice, supporting strategic planning, design and development, documentation, submission, negotiations, and program implementation. A seasoned professional in a wide range of roles—biopharmaceutical executive, principal consultant, and future government regulator—he was very methodical, strategic, and rigorous in his approach to the work that ParagonRx was doing. This was an important time in disease management, drug safety, and therapeutic risk management. Slatko led the team with a balanced perspective of what had to be done, how it could be done, and how to ensure it was done with scientific rigor.

Their original idea had been to improve the sales and value of medications by identifying how health-care providers could use particular products more effectively and safely. They thought of themselves as innovative pioneers on two fronts: adapting the application of prospective, systematic, human factors methods for evaluating pharmaceutical safety risks and developing effective risk-management intervention programs. As Fetterman said, their goal was to "make pharmaceutical products as effective and safe to use in the real world as they were demonstrated to be in clinical trials."

After the pair established their company in 2001, their business seesawed. They had a vision for what they were doing, yet growing a start-up company is never easy. Their first clients often required a specific project in support of their drug trials. But, as the entrepreneurs quickly learned, having a single client with a specific need is time consuming and not a good strategy for future growth. Later, as they became well known in the industry, demand for their services grew, with clients that ranged from multinational pharmaceutical manufacturers to specialized biotechnology companies and generic product manufacturers.

Then, in 2007, the Food and Drug Administration Amendments Act (FDAAA) granted the FDA the authority to require pharmaceutical companies to submit and implement a Risk Evaluation and Mitigation Strategy (REMS) if the FDA determined that this was necessary to ensure that a drug's benefits outweighed its risks. It would open an entirely new market space for ParagonRx, but there were many questions still to be answered, both about REMS and about how the growing company could take full advantage of this new opportunity.

When Slatko and Fetterman contacted me, the business was in transition. ParagonRx had a wonderful team of talented professionals, and the company had a proprietary systematic approach called RxFMEA®, adapted from aviation and other industries, that they applied to designing pharmaceutical risk management programs. This bottom-up assessment was a structured process that could be repeated regardless of the drug being developed. It promoted the disciplined identification of the kinds of failures that might occur, careful analysis of specific risk/hazard areas, proper documentation of sources and assumptions, and identification of interventions that could effectively manage the risks to an acceptable level.

For ParagonRx, this was the gold standard of how to apply a process to design, develop, and manage REMS for long-term success of a product in the market. Their application would help pharmaceutical companies and the FDA better identify and address unforeseen, undesired outcomes. "When regulators see this transparent process," Fetterman said, "negotiation can be based on facts and evidence, rather than on opinion and speculation." Yet their approach wasn't as easily understood or embraced by clients as he and Slatko had expected it to be.

We were engaged by ParagonRx to help them craft a

branding strategy, establish a marketing position, and better build their business so that their proprietary methodology, tools, and theory could become the standard for REMS. They wanted us to explore how the firm could help both the pharmaceutical industry address the REMS requirements and the FDA better evaluate the approaches being recommended through REMS. Both Slatko and Fetterman felt that observational research could help ParagonRx see itself and its methods through a new lens. They knew what they needed. They just weren't sure how to accomplish it on their own.

The Coumadin™ Experience

The two men had already had extensive careers before they established ParagonRx. Early on, Fetterman had led a pre-start-up safety assessment of a nuclear reactor. Then he spent a dozen years in pharmaceutical companies leading marketing for various cardiovascular products. He also managed operations for a consumer health start-up venture that was intended to commercialize premium nutritional supplements. He co-founded Empower Health, which offered health-plan services and technologies to improve clinical outcomes.

Slatko had both an MBA and an MD, and his career in major pharmaceutical companies focused on drug safety, medical services, and disease management development methodologies. For GlaxoSmithKline, he had led the company's US disease management division, improving the quality of care for asthma, migraines, smoking cessation, influenza, and other important clinical conditions.

He and Fetterman met when they were at DuPont Pharmaceuticals, where their challenge was to advance Coumadin, a blood-thinning product that many doctors were afraid to use.

Initially, physicians were very hesitant to prescribe the drug for elderly patients in danger of cardiogenic stroke, because the doctors felt that the parallel dangers of bleeding from the medication itself were not properly addressed.

Fetterman and Slatko participated in a team that used observational research and ethnography at physicians' practices to understand what the doctors did, how they prescribed alternatives such as aspirin to patients, and their risk-avoidance behaviors around Coumadin. They spent time as part of a team observing how patients actually used the product and noting which doctors were more proficient and comfortable with it, as compared with those physicians who were less proficient. They came to understand how powerful it was to actually watch what the doctors who were successfully managing many Coumadin patients were actually doing and not just asking them to tell you what they thought they were doing.

"What this experience showed was that physicians are, in general and appropriately, risk savvy," remembered Fetterman. "Given a product that has a defined patient benefit, but which also has dangers if not properly addressed, doctors tend to prescribe it very narrowly," he said. Adds Slatko: "We were taught as part of our physician oath to 'do no harm.'"

Out of the research, the team was able to develop CoumaCare™, a care management program that helped everyday clinicians become more proficient in the use of Coumadin for the care of more of their patients. As a result of this and other efforts, sales increased sevenfold over seven years, despite Coumadin being a forty-year-old product at the time! Undoubtedly, thousands of patients avoided strokes because physicians felt more comfortable prescribing for more patients when following certain processes and precautions evolved by their more experienced peers.

Ten years later, Fetterman and Slatko reconnected and founded ParagonRx. "We wanted to use the same methods to see which physicians were proficient in using complex medications and learn how to teach others to do the same," Fetterman explained. "It was less about safety than improved performance and marketing success. Most companies did not think they needed this. A few enlightened companies became our clients. We had to become more effective at communicating what we could do and how we could do it."

It wasn't that risk-mitigation strategies were new for the pharmaceutical industry or the FDA. In 2005, guidance for risk minimization action plans (RiskMAPs) had been provided to manufacturers to examine the scope of risk and look at who was at risk, the existence of treatment alternatives, preventability of adverse events through appropriate prescribing, and how the RiskMAP process could help reduce risk.

The evolution to REMS, however, opened up an entirely new market space. Slatko and Fetterman weren't quite sure how to build a business around it, though they already had published two books on the topic: *A Framework for Pharmaceutical Risk Management* (2003) and *Pharmaceutical Risk Management: Practical Applications* (2008). Given their experience with CoumaCare, they were open to an anthropological approach.

ParagonRx and REMS

I began, as we often do, by observing. For part of each week, we just hung out at the company. It was very interesting to sit in on meetings, work on strategic planning, watch the team develop proposals, and listen in on RxFMEA discussions. FMEA stands for "Failure Modes and Effects Analysis," which was one of the first systematic techniques for failure analysis, developed originally by reliability engineers in the military. ParagonRx added the "Rx" to brand its approach to evaluating and mitigating the risks associated with pharmaceutical products. We were searching for data about what they were telling clients, hoping the data would come together into a branding story that would resonate with this emerging market for REMS and create more demand for an evidence-based process. We were also observing the company's unique culture and ways of getting its business done. We had a year to work with the company; this approach is not designed to learn everything in a few moments but to see things evolve as employees go through their daily lives.

As we watched business come into ParagonRx—or not—we became fascinated by why it was so hard to convince clients to choose the company for a product's REMS. After all, ParagonRx was so good at its process, which was unique. Was the process that hard to imagine? Was the FDA making potential clients leery about how RxFMEA would meet their needs?

We listened as the management hired new salespeople, and we helped staff booths or set up dinners at conferences, which were wonderful opportunities to listen to prospective clients.

What we discovered underlined the fact that ParagonRx had a well-developed, documented, and effective approach. They were well-respected experts in the field of drug safety and marketing. They even had the beginnings of a distinctive and proprietary brand position at a time when the market space was just evolving.

As part of our research, we also went out to conduct culture probes and story-interviews among some of the company's key or prospective clients in large pharmaceutical and biotech firms, from Amgen and Covidien to Genentech and Sanofi. We were able to meet with leaders in the fields of drug safety and pharmacovigilance as well as in marketing and product development. It turned out that all of them were approaching the REMS problem from slightly different angles. We began to see that there was still a theoretical and practical vacuum waiting for someone to fill it with philosophy, methodologies, and tools to use to get REMS right.

For some of the drug and biotech companies, REMS was clearly a game changer. No longer was success just about having better marketing materials or more details about potential risks on TV spots. Rather, you were going to have to figure out what an effective risk-mitigation approach was and how well you were actually mitigating those risks. This wasn't going to stop after your drug was approved. You were going to have to ensure that it was working.

Further, REMS would require developing a collaborative process, something that was unfamiliar to these pharmaceutical companies, which more commonly were organized in self-contained functional silos, each with its own responsibilities. In the past, marketing usually didn't get involved with new medications until the end of the development process conducted and owned by clinical development. Now those teams were asked: How could they create better education for patients who were going to be taking the drug so they would have the knowledge and understanding they needed to reduce the risks?

As one interviewee observed, "We have to socialize this through the organization . . . [REMS] was not a deliverable. People didn't know what to do with this yet."

Fetterman admitted, "I underappreciated this. Our process and the RxFMEA research are not just objective findings. We are helping organizations do what they have to do. Not just check a box."

That was where ParagonRx could come in. The company

could help define the industry's approach to an ill-defined, emerging process that was intended to have major transformative benefits for drug manufacturers and those taking the prescribed drugs.

Connecting the Data Dots for the Team

Interestingly—and not unexpectedly—tension rose as I shared the insights from these observations and interviews. The ParagonRx team was not sure how best to respond. Typically they tried to protect what they did and how they did it, often claiming that while ParagonRx had the solution, the prospective client just didn't get it.

Eventually it became clear that telling clients what ParagonRx had to offer was not always done with enough clarity and simplicity. Indeed, I was endlessly fascinated as I listened to panels of doctors and scientists at conferences discuss the problem of risk mitigation but ignore the solutions that were at hand. The idea that there was an RxFMEA process available to provide a rigorous, systematic approach was simply not well known. We began to work on the storytelling side of this process, converting what we had learned into action.

Both prospective and current clients needed to understand ParagonRx's unique advantages and expertise and how these could provide solutions far bigger than simply getting that box checked off. Gradually, we helped Fetterman, Slatko, and the team at ParagonRx adapt their story—stating clearly all the reasons why they were the best or the only.

One of the results was a webinar series through which the folks at ParagonRx could tell their story in a sustainable way that the industry could most easily grasp. This became the

ParagonRx Beacon, broadcasting the process and the latest in that process in a way that was easily understood and quickly transmitted. At one point, a large pharmaceutical organization had thirty team members watching those webinars together in a single room so they could use it as their training program.

With these webinars, new blogs, the two groundbreaking books, and a lot of good press, ParagonRx soon positioned itself as the thought leader in the field. It was actually a perfect spot for them.

One new client came to ParagonRx through the webinars, and when we interviewed them about how they found and chose the company, they were very open with us: "One of our staff watches your webinars. So when I asked the group who I should look at to help with a REMS problem, he immediately said ParagonRx. We didn't even know who they were or what they did. But that was a great educational method to get our folks familiar with you before we even knew we needed you."

Fetterman and Slatko knew their methods were effective. They just didn't understand how difficult it was for prospective clients to adopt new practices and build them into the solution. Their approach was not merely a product to be sold; a deep trust also had to be built. In some cases, ParagonRx actually became the outsourced solution for pharmaceutical companies that then didn't have to develop their own skills all at once.

Moving Forward and On

In 2010, just as we were about to complete our work, ParagonRx was acquired by inVentiv Health, an integrated group of discrete companies that are experts in bringing drugs to market and supporting all phases of the product lifecycle. Acquired by a private equity firm, it is today a global, top-tier clinical and commercial professional services company. The brand positioning for inVentiv Health is clear: "By combining the best strategic brains in the biopharmaceutical industry with the latest technologies, we've worked to eliminate the roadblocks, territories, fences, hand-offs, and gaps that can hinder the efficiency and speed at which you bring products into the hands of the people who need them most." This seemed like a perfect fit for ParagonRx to gain access to greater resources for its own growth by teaming with other inVentiv Health companies to serve their common clients.

Within inVentiv Health, ParagonRx remained focused on dramatic regulatory changes both in the United States and globally. Said Fetterman, "Regulators are under pressure to speed review of new medical products while simultaneously improving safety. As a consequence, drug developers and device makers planning for a successful review must be proactive in assuring optimal and safe use of products before the products come up for review. The focus today is on enhanced pharmacovigilance, putting preventions in place before any regulatory body requires it."

> "EVEN THOUGH WE UNDERSTOOD
> ETHNOGRAPHIC RESEARCH AND HOW WE
> HAD TO SEE THIS FROM OUR CUSTOMERS'
> PERSPECTIVES, WE DIDN'T."

In late 2012, as the FDA itself began to recognize the power of a more evidence-based design approach to REMS, the agency recruited Slatko to head the Office of Medication

Error Prevention and Risk Management. He remains with the FDA to this day.

Early in 2015, Fetterman left ParagonRx to take on other challenges. He remembered how seeing things through a new lens had changed the company. "Even though we understood ethnographic research and how we had to see this from our customers' perspectives, we didn't. We didn't step outside ourselves to see what we were doing. In fact it was less about what [the customers] needed and more about what we offered. We had designed our RxFMEA process and knew what we could do but didn't really know how to position this for what they needed from us."

Business today is less about selling a product or a solution and far more about helping clients solve their problems collaboratively, bringing in expertise that complements what they have, and making them better able to actually not need you any longer. Our experience with ParagonRx was really a collaborative relationship in which we both were stepping in and out of the company to see it from the perspective of their clients and from the culture of ParagonRx itself. The result was our ability to forge a new story for ParagonRx that fit them well, while matching up remarkably closely to the unmet needs of their clients as their times were changing.

Lessons Learned from ParagonRx for Your Company

We are often asked to work with early stage or start-up companies. While we enjoy their challenges, we have also found that they are frequently trying to build a factory in hopes that someone will buy their product. This is almost what ParagonRx did.

Here are some lessons you can leverage for growth, whether you are a start-up or an established company.

1. Don't assume you know what your prospective clients need.

   When we began working with ParagonRx, they were sure that the RxFMEA was just what their clients needed. In actuality, their clients weren't yet sure what the new regulations' requirements were, so the RxFMEA was not a sure thing at all. What about your future customers for your new products, services, or solutions? Are you building it and hoping that customers will come? This is a common mistake, and you can fix it using the same approach as ParagonRx. First, go out to your clients and listen to what they are worried about and how they are scoping out solutions to new unmet needs. Second, resist the urge to design a solution and hand it back to your clients. Instead, collaborate with them to design a solution that best fits their definition of the problem.

2. Become a thought leader.

   Whenever a new market emerges, it is often searching for thought leadership, for someone at the helm who is ready with answers to uncertainties. Could you be that thought leader? A book, a blog, and speaking engagements are great ways to launch you into that role. Better yet, bring together others who can help co-brand you and share the stage.

3. Selling your products might need some innovative techniques.

   When you think of Post-its, Purell, WD-40, and even

Nespresso, you realize that great products aren't always adopted immediately, even in today's fast-paced market. For your company, test a range of different sales strategies to build trial users and capture endorsements, then leverage their stories to build enthusiasm, viral or otherwise. If your product is really "cool" and opening up a new market space, you are going to have to create demand, not just satisfy current demand—if there is any current demand. Test, test, test . . . refine your strategy as things start to work.

4. Use ethnography to observe and innovate.
Even though Jeff Fetterman and Gary Slatko were well versed in the theory and use of ethnographic research, it was hard for them to do observational research on their own business. If this sounds familiar, you might consider finding anthropologists who can help you. But remember: Never outsource your eyes. Stay close to the researcher so you yourself can see things with fresh eyes.

DON'T ASSUME YOU KNOW WHAT YOUR PROSPECTIVE CLIENTS NEED.

....

CHAPTER 9

CENTENARY COLLEGE

DR. KENNETH L. HOYT was sitting in his first board meeting at his new job as president of Centenary College in New Jersey when someone entered the room and handed him a note that read, "An airplane has crashed into the Trade Center in NY . . . we think you need to do something different." It was September 11, 2001, and planes had just crashed into New York's World Trade Center. Many Centenary students, faculty, and staff had family or friends in the buildings, or thought they did, and there was no way to know what had happened to them.

There was no known "best practice" for this type of situation. Hoyt called everyone into the chapel, and together they prayed and waited. Cell phones brought the news that all but one of their loved ones had been some other place that day. As the faculty and students drew close during that crisis, Hoyt realized that this was a great place to be, even though the college was struggling to find its way. Yes, there was a lot of tension and friction, but the Centenary family was able to rally together. Could they also find a way to restore the vitality of the college and help it grow?

When Dr. Hoyt had arrived at Centenary College two weeks earlier, he was coming to a college in serious financial trouble. Centenary was known as a two-year woman's finishing school with an equitation program and a limited course curriculum focused on teacher education. Enrollment was declining, annual deficits were staggering, and Centenary was unsophisticated at raising funds. Facilities were in a distressed state and no new facilities had been built since the 1960s. For most students, the college was their only choice, and they planned to transfer to other colleges as soon as possible.

Centenary was also a bit off the beaten path in the Kittatinny Mountains, fifty-two miles west of New York City, thirty-five miles south of the Delaware Water Gap National Recreation Area, and twenty-six miles northeast of Easton, Pennsylvania, and the Lehigh Valley. The surrounding region is beautiful but sparsely populated, meaning that students had to come from elsewhere in the state and the region for the college to thrive. There was little to differentiate this former girls' college from many other similar schools in nearby Pennsylvania and New Jersey.

The Challenge in Context

Centenary had undergone some huge changes in the previous two decades. When Dr. Stephanie Bennett-Smith became president of Centenary in 1984, she was only the second woman to hold the presidency of a United Methodist Church–affiliated college or university. With a vision of creating a Swarthmore for New Jersey, Dr. Bennett-Smith strengthened the institution during her fifteen years as president. She took it co-educational in 1988, expanded its international programs, and revised the curriculum to incorporate required community service. She also established the graduate program, began an adult learning program, and completed the first-ever modest fundraising campaign in the college's history, mostly for the renovation of the old main building.

However, as Bennett-Smith was trying to reinvigorate the culture, Centenary's student population stalled at about seven hundred students, and staying financially viable was becoming a challenge.

Ken Hoyt was the kind of take-charge yet collaborative individual who was really needed in a turnaround situation. Fifty-something, the quiet Midwesterner exuded confidence and a sense of command. He was open to ideas, yet very clear about what he knew had to be done. He made you want to be part of his team so you could help him restore hope to the college community and help it grow.

Hoyt had been recruited to Centenary after sixteen years as the president of Ohio's consortium of private colleges and universities. In that role, he pushed these colleges to adapt new directions using business process redesign and cost-saving collaborations. He was a visionary who demonstrated an ability to help them rethink their business models, and he was an accomplished change agent, actively working with his thirty-five member colleges to transform their organizations so they could sustain their growth in efficient and effective ways. Hoyt hadn't exactly been looking to move from Ohio to New Jersey to serve a small college where he could apply what he had learned working with a group of colleges. But when the recruiter called, he was intrigued.

The Pain of Change

As we know all too well, it is hard for anyone to shed one vision of an organization and its future and replace it with a new one, much less trust the new one to be a better solution than the older one that had failed them. Change is challenging. But sometimes there is little choice. We often say, if you want to change, have a crisis—and indeed, it was crisis time for Centenary.

> IT IS HARD FOR ANYONE TO SHED ONE VISION OF AN ORGANIZATION AND ITS FUTURE AND REPLACE IT WITH A NEW ONE. CHANGE IS CHALLENGING.

It didn't take long for Hoyt to identify a number of problem areas. First, the school's public persona was that of a two-year girls' finishing school with horses. The only thing that was still true about that statement was the horse program. In fact, Centenary had a well-respected college equestrian program, but that was hardly enough to attract a viable student body. It did have a well-regarded teachers' training program and several career-oriented majors.

However, the administration was poorly designed for either recruiting students or retaining them. From a recruitment perspective, the college was virtually unknown among high school guidance counselors. That meant recruiters had to do a double sale, first explaining what Centenary was and then following up with why students should consider it. There was no systematic high-school recruiting process or administrative system to support one.

Moreover, retention rates were terrible. When Hoyt arrived in 2001, only about fifty percent of the first-year students returned to become sophomores. That was well below the national average of seventy-six percent. The financial impact of such a student churn was serious, and the completion rates were hardly great endorsements for the value of a Centenary education.

Although the school had launched a program for non-traditional (adult) students, it was still a small part of the college's focus, about two-hundred part-time students. Yes, non-traditional students were being recruited, but classes were taught in the traditional fashion and took place on campus and at one off-campus location. Old models of teaching and learning still dominated the college's thinking, which did not work for adults seeking accelerated learning models.

All of the innovations that were taking place across the United States to expand college programs for non-traditional students, and for the business environment that needed those students, were being ignored at Centenary.

Dr. Hoyt's Strategy

Hoyt began to attack these challenges by promoting some excellent talent and hiring others.

Then Hoyt turned to the outmoded facilities and lack of investment in the campus. By 2002, he had completed a Campus Master Plan to take stock of the college's campus requirements, planning for additional acreage, a student and performing arts center, suite-style campus housing, and the renovation of athletic facilities that had been built in the 1950s for a women's college and did not meet current NCAA standards. He also realized that without an investment in technology, the school would fall behind what was expected from a leader in educating a new generation of students who had grown up in a digital world.

One of the best ways to fund these changes was to capture the revenue that was leaving the school due to weak retention and to create new revenue streams. Increasing the retention rate from fifty-four percent to eighty percent would translate to an additional fourteen million dollars to the bottom-line revenues. The now reconfigured and rapidly expanding Centenary adult program also added eight million to the bottom line each year, helping to grow Centenary from eighteen million dollars to forty-three million dollars in operations.

While he worked on recruiting the best permanent faculty and administrators, Hoyt also brought on a number of consultants, myself included, to help rethink and rebuild the college.

The Missing Pieces

We were introduced to Centenary in 2002, early in our consulting business, and Centenary was a perfect launchpad for us. Our assignment was twofold: First, the college needed someone to clarify the ideal "Centenary Student." What kind of person would thrive in this small liberal arts college, which was investing in new programs to better meet his or her needs? Second, could we convert that research into brand positioning that differentiated Centenary from other schools, and then help build the brand, market the college, and create demand for the institution? We approached these tasks very much like an anthropological research project.

> WE NEEDED TO EXPERIENCE THE COLLEGE AS IF WE WERE STUDENTS, TO UNDERSTAND IT AS IF WE WERE THEIR FAMILIES, AND TO VISUALIZE IT THROUGH THE EYES OF HIGH SCHOOL GUIDANCE COUNSELORS OR A BUSINESS'S HUMAN RESOURCE STAFF.

It was clear from the beginning that there was so much change going on all over the campus that we had to be innovative in our approach. Before the college could easily answer the question "Why Centenary?" we needed to probe deeply into its personality. Certainly this needed more than a survey or even focus-group research. We needed to experience the college as if we were students, to understand it as if we were their families, and to visualize it through the eyes of high school guidance counselors or a business's human resource staff. Without that, we weren't sure we could create a realistic story that could generate applications. There was no way around it: We had to get to know Centenary as if we were living there.

In New Jersey in 2001, more than seventy-five percent of students left the state to go to college. After 9/11, students' college selection process began to favor institutions closer to home, a fact that helped Centenary's turnaround. For a good strong liberal college, it seemed on the surface that there would be a lot of potential prospects for Centenary. I wasn't quite sure why applications were not stronger and applicants more interested in attending. I could look at the data, but it really didn't explain where the challenges lay.

We began looking at where the college had been focused and how that had evolved in the 1990s, the decade before Hoyt came on board. It turned out that Centenary had a good, if limited, reputation for training K–12 teachers. It was also trying to add additional liberal arts and career-oriented programs that it could afford to support and for which there was need or interest. These were growing slowly.

When Hoyt came in, he launched the Centenary Experience: Student-Centered Learning and Unparalleled Service. He also crafted a new core curriculum and incorporated a new First Year Experience Program, which would bond new students together and increase their loyalty to the institution. One of the great eventual benefits of the first-year program was its impact on retention. From 2001 to 2008, Hoyt hosted every new freshman at the president's house for dinner, so he could ask each student what needed to change to improve the college. At first, students would report they had enrolled in Centenary but planned to transfer. As things improved, the students dining with Dr. Hoyt and his wife Marcia reported that Centenary was their first-choice institution and they felt welcome and at home.

In the meantime, though, these changes had led to widespread frustration and then anger among the faculty and staff. Despite the fact that the college was struggling, few people wanted to trust Hoyt and embrace these early-stage changes, whether they were the new first-year curriculum or non-traditional programs for adult learners. We needed them to trust us as well.

To ease that process, I hung out a lot all over the campus. I went to classes and observed, trying to pick up the essence of the student experience. These were not easy times for the faculty. The millennials who were now entering college had grown up digital, and their helicopter parents often dropped in unexpectedly to advocate for their son or daughter. Faculty members were frustrated by students' lack of ability to do projects individually. These were soccer kids; if something wasn't organized as a team sport, they didn't really know how to play. And although it was clear that faculty members often had a hard time figuring out their new students, they nevertheless taught the way they always had, and expected students to act like the students they were used to.

As I watched faculty during meetings or listened to students, we noticed some traits that Centenary shared with other colleges. They were aware that things were changing, but insisted that the way their faculty taught students was the best way. They were working really hard to prove that they didn't need the changes. They considered their present situation to be someone else's problem.

Ironically, the teachers were doing a great deal that *was* different and that created real value for students. We began to refer to this process as an "education designed around you." As we watched classroom activity and after-class engagement, the distinctions from other colleges stood out: This was a small school, and individual students received a lot of attention and often were the focus of concern. Students spent a great deal of time with faculty in their offices. The conversations were rich and deep, and the shared experiences were, for many students, transformational. That message, though, had yet to be packaged into a consistent brand of education that the college could leverage.

From the faculty, we kept hearing a repeated theme: There was tremendous pride in how they taught their student teachers to "teach to how students learn." Their methodology was very experiential and tailored to multiple intelligences and learning styles. This was actually an unrecognized "theme song" and pertained as much to the way the Centenary faculty went about their business as it did to how their graduates were going to teach their K–12 students. Students in majors other than education received instruction in much the same way.

As for the students, whether they were eighteen-year-olds or working professionals returning to school, they were very articulate about what they were searching for in their education. Attending a small college in a remote area of New Jersey was not an easy decision for a high school graduate or a returning student. Neither was it an obvious choice for someone seeking an advanced degree.

As we listened, we could hear core values and aspirations

begin to emerge in the storytelling. The students were very focused on "belonging" and being "part of something that was 'becoming.'" Even the non-traditional students wanted to feel a part of "The Centenary Experience: An Education Designed Around You." They liked the new energy that they found on the campus. In particular, students really related to the first-year experience as a transformative one. It seemed to take them beyond who they were when they arrived and helped them bond with their fellow students, just as it was designed to do.

Centenary's program for adult students had also become more attuned to a need for flexibility and family/work balance. The program was expanded to two sites in areas close to where many of these students worked, and it began to offer real value in an accelerated format that allowed people working full time to also be full-time students.

As part of our process, we went out to work with the team that was creating the non-traditional programs to introduce them to businesses around the state. To do this, we interviewed potential students about their unmet needs and tried to anticipate where Centenary was on track or off in program development. It made sense both to the prospective businesses and the students to ask a lot of questions of these two groups and then listen for how to structure a non-traditional program so it could accommodate the needs of divergent groups.

This was not an entirely new venture; it had been launched earlier and was being revamped by Hoyt. He was restructuring Centenary's Center for Adult and Professional Studies (CAPS) under their Council for Adult and Experiential Learning (CAEL) Standards. This program would be recognized in 2007 by the National Academic Advising Associations (NACADA) for innovation in adult learning.

We also worked closely with the director of admissions,

Diane Finnan, to better understand how she could penetrate the high school student market. As we went out with her staff to visit schools and college fairs, it was easy to understand their challenge. The guidance counselors didn't know much about Centenary and had little time to learn. Diane and her team members were terrific, but they needed a simple, strong story to sell and a way to make it easier for the guidance counselors to identify the right students for the college.

I sometimes wondered if anyone really cared about what we were doing. When we started, most people on campus thought it was sort of nice to have someone hanging around. At times we were the folks they vented to. At other times we became a useful third party to bounce ideas off of.

But over time, as Centenary evolved, the new things on campus became tone-changers. We could watch the shifts in values, beliefs, and even behaviors—the culture—of both faculty and students. We also began to see something unique at Centenary that could differentiate it from the competition and make it clear why students should consider it as a viable option.

Building the Story

What was the story, then? This was a college that "taught you the way you learned" and did it in a very experiential, team-focused way. Plus, Centenary was being rebuilt in both the physical and the cultural sense. New buildings and new programs—particularly the first-year experience—were concrete evidence of the abstract shifts in their core values, beliefs, and ways of doing things.

ONCE WE SETTLED ON THIS MESSAGE, WE HAD TO FIGURE OUT HOW TO MAKE IT COME ALIVE.

Once we settled on this message, we had to figure out how to make it come alive. We had to develop marketing strategies and brand design and development. We actually could not find another college, or even a teachers' college, that was doing the same thing or promoting itself in this way. "We Teach You the Way You Learn" was an honest statement. The college was really doing this. And it was working to help students to stay in college, to graduate, and to succeed afterward.

The major branding and marketing campaign had another great element to add to the mix. Centenary began to lead as an early adopter in the use of the Internet and wireless technology in its teaching and learning environment, and it implemented a new wireless laptop initiative. Laptops were provided for all faculty, staff, and students.

It seems hard to believe now, but at the time Centenary was only one of one hundred such institutions in North America that gave laptops to every student. In 2005, it was selected by both Intel and Forbes as one of the Top 50 Wireless Campuses in the United States. That was a huge differentiator and was symbolic of how the college would become an innovator in higher education. It also opened up an entirely new way to teach those students, engage them in the process, and build a community around their interests and needs.

We launched a major marketing push with widespread advertising throughout New Jersey to build the brand identity and shift attitudes toward the college among students, parents, and high school counselors. Along with this strategic campaign came new logos, graphic design, and marketing materials building on the New American College concept. The New American Colleges were selective, small to midsize independent colleges and universities dedicated to the "purposeful integration of liberal education, professional studies, and civic

engagement." At the time, it was a new idea built on the prem-
ise that students should learn through hands-on, project-based
experiences in order to enable them to connect theory to practice. With programs designed to directly tie classroom learning to real-world situations, New American Colleges were
also deeply committed to civic responsibility, whether local,
national, or global in nature.

All the materials describing Centenary shared a common
thread to heighten understanding of why this was a college
education that students should consider and how the college
taught them in an individualized way. The college became repo-
sitioned as a nationally recognized small independent college
that taught you the way you best learned.

This kind of marketing and brand building is not just nice
but also essential to make an experience like a college "live,"
so prospects can "feel" it before they even see it. Now that
we finally had the story, we had to develop the tools to tell it.
"The Centenary College Experience: An Education Designed
Around You" worked.

Even though this was 2002, we knew that without a website, Centenary was going to struggle to recruit students. We
built the college's first website in 2004 with one of their students who was learning how to code. It was really a start-up
site; no one was sure how to build one or what should be on it.
Resources were limited, too, but the talented coder was typical
of the school's can-do student base, and together he and I used
the opportunity to brand the college online. It fit perfectly with
what we were there to do.

Since then, of course, I've recognized how valuable website
design and development and the building process is for an organization. Crafting website architecture requires that an enterprise see itself as others will see it. As the student and I created

Centenary's site map and wireframe as well as the graphic design, we identified those on campus who could really articulate how things at the college were connected or what students would want to know about the school, its programs, and the way students were taught there. The site became a terrific vehicle for solidifying the brand positioning and engaging the faculty and staff in how to express it.

Moving On

We worked with Centenary from 2002 to 2006, and though the results were still emerging when our assignment ended, the future direction was clear. By then, Centenary had become the fastest-growing college or university in New Jersey, having increased undergraduate, adult, and graduate enrollment to 3,200 in seven years, while maintaining a good financial picture. As for the retention strategy, it was found that for beginning, full-time freshman students going through the first-year experience, retention rates increased by more than thirty percent and graduation rates by twenty percent. As a result of its success, Centenary was selected to participate as one of ninety colleges in John Gardner's First Year Foundations of Excellence Program in 2007.

Meanwhile, because of the need to expand, the school launched The Campaign for Centenary College. Hoyt was able to secure $45.5 million in new resources for the facilities, programs, and endowment, securing a lead gift of eighteen million dollars, which is the largest gift in Centenary's history. With campaign funds, he also constructed a thirty-million-dollar student and performing arts center, a new technology classroom building, all new athletic facilities, and two new suite-style housing complexes, and secured an additional twenty acres of land for the college, a fifty percent increase in land area.

Dr. Hoyt left Centenary in 2009, having finished the turnaround he had envisioned. He continues to work with independent colleges and universities through his consulting firm, The Higher Education Practice, LLC, to help them assess their strengths and weaknesses and reposition themselves for growth.

By 2012, Centenary's enrollment was steady at around 2,576 students: 1,340 traditional full-time and 110 part-time undergraduate students, and 1,126 adult accelerated and graduate students. It continues to offer undergraduate and graduate studies. What is particularly interesting is that more than a decade later, those on campus say they still remember the work we did and the way it generated growth. Most of all, they recall how it gave them a place in the state where they could be successful and still be themselves.

Lessons Learned from Centenary College for Your Business

The world of private colleges today is under siege from many fronts, and though Centenary's future was not solidified by the changes Dr. Hoyt put into place, its financial and student turnaround provided a foundation for it to continue to expand effectively. More importantly, Hoyt gave the college something that your organization might find of great value: a new way to think about its role for students and society. The college's mission was to produce well-prepared and educated students who could successfully thrive throughout their adult lives and continue to learn. For your organization, what might this mean for you? Here are four things to consider.

1. What are you really doing? Yes, teaching, but
   what and why?

   A recurring theme we hear today from businesses and corporations, and which Centenary certainly heard, is that
   colleges are not preparing students for the jobs of tomorrow. While a liberal arts education might provide students
   with a firm foundation of knowledge, the fast-changing
   skills needed for "knowledge workers" is outpacing the academic process of higher educational institutions. Is it time
   for you to go hang out with your students and listen to
   their views of the world, their stories—from their perspectives? Perhaps you need to build your institution's mission
   backwards, starting with the needs of businesses and the
   types of people they need to hire. At the very least, rethink
   "What are we teaching and why?" If you are not a college,
   the question is still very relevant. Who are you serving and
   how well are you doing it?

2. Is your business model the right one for the
   future? What is the data telling you?

   Regardless of what type of business you're in, you have
   abundant data. What are the stories that data is telling you?
   Are you looking at it properly and evaluating its meaning
   for your business model? While anthropologists want to
   help you understand the "meaning" of that abundant data,
   you might begin yourself to examine it with fresh eyes.
   What exactly is it telling you and how could this help you
   rethink your business model for the future?

3. What is the life cycle of your relationship with your customers?

Is it a single product purchase or a lifelong engagement over their "buyer's journey?"

Are you ready to step back and look at your engagement with your customers over their buyer's journey? This might be a good time to realize that there is a prequel and a sequel to that purchase and to think about how these two steps affect your relationship with that user or consumer or business purchaser. If you map the sequence, what kind of revenue streams might be awaiting you and your business that you are ignoring today?

4. Business stories change. How are you changing yours?

As Hoyt was changing Centenary College's core offering and student experience, he knew that his brand and the stories being told about that brand had to change as well. This might be a good time for you to rethink your business, the way you live your brand internally, and how you should be telling your new story to the markets you want to serve. Remember that people are storytellers. If you don't tell them the new story, they will make one up, usually based on the past experiences they have had with you. Changing the story is not easy, but it is extremely necessary and must be done through all media channels.

CHAPTER 10

....

CREATING A NEW VISION

OVER THE YEARS, as I have worked with CEOs, I realized that I had to stop asking them my opening workshop question: "Are you, an innovative leader, helping your company remain competitive in a fast-changing business environment?"

> WHEN I ASKED CEOS TO TELL ME A
> SINGLE SUCCESS STORY ABOUT HOW
> THEIR COMPANY HAD INNOVATED,
> OR HOW THEY HAD DONE SOMETHING
> BEYOND A PRODUCT IMPROVEMENT
> OR INCREMENTAL INNOVATION, THEY
> WOULD STAMMER AND STUTTER.

The CEOs would all raise their hands and go on to tell me how innovative their organization was and how much they encouraged and fostered empowerment among their staff. When I asked them to tell me a single success story about how their company had innovated, however, or how they had done something beyond a product improvement or incremental innovation, they would stammer and stutter. They wanted to be seen as innovators. And they wanted their company to thrive as an innovative organization with a leadership position in their industry and cool new products and services. But far too often, their actions were more about the promise than the performance.

> STAYING THE COURSE, EMBRACING CORE COMPETENCIES, AND SEEKING A SHARE OF A STATIC MARKET ARE NO LONGER VIABLE OPTIONS.

Innovation is often just a great big word that is almost a cli-ché. When it comes to actually innovating, people have limited training and are too risk-averse to do it effectively. Many CEOs know how to run a company, but they rarely have the skills or talent to change one. Yet the need for innovation in business today is ubiquitous. As change challenges all companies at every level, simply staying the course, embracing core competencies, and seeking a share of a static market are no longer viable options.

The obstacles to creating innovative corporate cultures and sustaining them emerge from the very things that were often the lifeblood of companies founded by entrepreneurs who could somehow see opportunities where others could not. From those founders' visions came flexibility, ingenuity, and exciting success stories.

The companies described in the previous case studies had energetic periods like that during their development. And their current leaders knew well how the enterprises had emerged and surged, but they weren't sure how to keep their products and services from lagging or failing in the marketplace. Are the times that different now from when these companies were founded? In many ways, the answer is yes.

Today the difficulty is due to a number of disparate elements that come together to set up roadblocks to corporate creativity and agility. Companies develop their own cultures, which keep them operating. But then, the stability and structure that has typically been necessary to grow the company becomes the major barrier to allowing new ideas to rise to the surface or to become testable innovations. It becomes difficult to set up a process or support for risk-taking "intrapreneurs"— those entrepreneurs inside an organization—that allows them to convert those ideas to effective innovations.

Because of these internal corporate obstacles, we frequently get calls to help companies rethink their business and uncover future opportunities. Some of these leaders need help to see, feel, and think in new ways about their well-established products and processes or the trends that are challenging their business. What they *really* need to do, though, is to put a process of discovery—of anthropology—into their business model, so that innovation happens routinely, not episodically. They need to think about change as something "we do here," not something you avoid until there is a crisis.

In other cases, the resistance to change comes from the power of a family firm to challenge the organization's ability to adapt to a changing business environment. Frequently family firms are so focused on interpersonal relationships and "teamwork" that they forget how to step back and reevaluate the status quo. In one situation that we researched, the company had forty-nine family members working in the organization. New opportunities were emerging all around them, but they ignored them in order to (as they saw it) protect the family and their respective roles. Perhaps they were also protecting their illusion that things would return to the way they used to be, eliminating any reason to change at all.

Ninety percent of US firms operate as family firms or firms run by families. Building a culture inside those firms to sustain innovation and build corporate agility is critically important if they are going to respond to today's accelerated pace of change. It might feel safer to stand behind "what we do here," but the poor success rate of family firms over multiple generations proves it is a losing proposition to do so.

Indeed, research shows us that "approximately, only 30 percent of all family-owned businesses survive into the second generation, and only 12 percent will survive into the third. Surprisingly, only three percent of all family businesses operate at the fourth generation and beyond. Therefore, making it to the fourth generation is very rare."[1] Embracing simple ways to step outside the tried and true might make the pain of change more tolerable for those firms and the families who want to protect and grow them, while at the same time providing more business possibilities for those firms.

As we saw in Chapter 1, part of the reason people—and firms—are slow to change is that our brains resist change. We create a mind map that sorts incoming reality to conform to what it thinks is real and then discards those tidbits of information—call-center inquiries, email requests, one-off client requirements—that don't fit our basic business. It doesn't matter who we are or what our business is; we all have a hard time seeing things that are right before us, unless we are constantly on the lookout for disconnects and inconsistencies.

So how did the companies in the preceding chapters manage to transform their businesses? Not easily. In those cases, they called on an outsider—me—to help open their minds to new ideas and possibilities.

It's interesting to note that these case studies shared certain characteristics. First, there were crises, real or perceived, that many of these companies had to deal with: Something was "stuck;" growth had stalled; award-winning products were not selling; and the marketplace had changed drastically. Whatever the reason for the crisis or its size or scope, the pressure was building. Ironically, that is often the perfect time to change.

Second, many of these companies had recently welcomed a new leader who was hired to rethink the business and how it was being run. When a new CEO or general manager arrives, it often prompts a move to step back and look at the "ways we do things here." The leaders all needed new ideas and ways to change their businesses. Even entrepreneurs Jeff Fetterman and Jim Riley had to create new markets for themselves. The transformation process often hinges on the need for a company to bring in a new leader to reimagine the business.

New managers may be caught, however, between the organization's desire to integrate them into the established culture (and show why there's no real need to change) and its need to transform itself or adapt its products, services, and culture to new business environments. A new leader has to have the ability to see things with fresh eyes without seeming to be just a "weird" outsider whose ideas "won't work here." And they often need a hand in helping the current team learn how to step out of their own habits and see things with fresh eyes themselves.

In all of these situations, there was the need for a new tool kit to get employees and management throughout the organization to stand back, look at themselves from different perspectives, and understand how changes can take place even among staff members who have been doing things the same way for a long time. Often that means turning the most recalcitrant employee into the biggest fan of transformation and convincing die-hards that they, too, can change.

When I worked with the folks at Benjamin Obdyke, longtime employees at a medical center in the Midwest, and established faculty at Centenary College, there was a constant undercurrent of unrest. While staff members might have realized they had to do something differently, few wanted to or knew how. What convinced them most often, however, were things they themselves heard or saw. In the end, engagement, as the CEOs and presidents all found out, is not about words—encouraging or threatening ones—or carrots and sticks. It is all about creating and using experiential opportunities. Call it "active learning," which we know from pedagogical studies is really the best way to learn.

You cannot ignore the role (and the challenge) of demographics. New young hires behave differently than those who did their jobs previously. Similarly, clients may have new staff members who are changing the way they do business. Customers may now be buying your products or services in ways that are, at times, hard to imagine.

In the medical industry, for example, we worked with anesthesiologists who were having a tough time accommodating the needs of both baby-boomer doctors and those newly out of medical school. They all spoke English, but you wouldn't have known it. The doctors valued different things, had different work styles, and challenged each other in ways that made building the next generation of the practice very difficult. That was compounded by the fact that the patients from different generations were equally different in their loyalties, expectations, trust, and needs.

To be sure, changing demographics can open up new markets and opportunities; that was the case with TELERx. Other times, demographics present new problems. A financial services

The power of the strategy—particularly when it is one designed to open new markets, create demand, and transform an industry—is how it helps those employees better embrace the overall vision and see how the roles they play become part of a bigger story. If you can step back and watch for emerging trends, demographic patterns, and innovative technologies, you could find yourself opening new markets before they become old. You can look to the future. But to envision yours, you must get out of your office and stop trying to *imagine* what is happening. Go exploring. See what is really there for yourself, and get your teammates to do that with you.

Customers are trying to tell you something. It is time to hear them.

When you apply anthropological tools to your business, you become a partner with a particular type of explorer. Some final thoughts:

- We tinker, test, and are always observing to see with fresh eyes.

- We fail early and often, and learn from the failures, since we expect to have them.

- We spend a surprising amount of time not knowing the answer to the challenge at hand. But that is OK, since we assume no one knows all the answers. That is why we are on this adventure.

And so we forge ahead, delighted in our curiosity and comfortable with our own uncertainty. We truly believe there are possibilities awaiting us—we only need to see them.

....

1 "Family Business Stats," JSA Advising. http://www.jsaadvising.com/facts -figures-2

ACKNOWLEDGMENTS

AS I WAS preparing to write this portion of *On the Brink*, I read over some famous book acknowledgments and was amused at how many different ways authors chose to say thank you. And then I wondered, how would I say it when I came to the end of my book?

My gratitude makes answering that question easy. I'm in just the very best place to be right now. I'm ending a book that took far too long to write, rewrite, edit, and re-edit. All along the way, I was compelled by my sense that what we were doing might really matter, that we could help the people whom we've come to know well, and that we could help CEOs actually do the things that they desperately needed to do. Throughout this endeavor—pushing me at times, hugging me at others, never wavering—I had a great team of fans who took this book to the finish. Let me tell you about them.

There is Mary Louise Ball—ML to all of us. She copyedited so many times that often neither of us was sure which version of which story we were telling. It is only because of her great skills and joyful laugh that we got the book to the publisher in a form that almost made sense.

Then there is Joan Tapper. Joan is the developmental editor who took apart my book and put it back together again into something my readers would actually like to read.

My publisher, Greenleaf Book Group, has a terrific team of talent that has guided me along the way. How lucky I was to meet Tanya Hall, CEO of Greenleaf, at a Vistage event.

I must also acknowledge the wonderful chairs and members of Vistage International and The Executive Committee (TEC) in the US and Canada. They continue to invite me to share my "Change Matters: How to Find New Market Space" and other workshops to help their members find ways to see their businesses through a "fresh lens." Many of the case studies in the book come from Vistage members who became my clients. These are terrific organizations to which I am truly indebted.

At the beginning was Jim Wade, a dear friend and editor, who always kept saying, "Andi, you have a great book here. Finish it." Well, Jim, I finally finished it.

And through it all, my husband, Andy, and my daughters, Alexandra and Rachel, were my constant companions. I met Andy when I was nineteen. He asked me what I wanted to be. I said, "An anthropologist." His immediate response was so cool: "Be an anthropologist, and I will always be here for you." So I did and so he was, always there for me.

When my daughters were four and five, I took them along with me to the rustic Greek island of Antiparos where I continued my post-doctoral research. Somehow they hung in there with me. They learned to ride donkeys, figured out how to swim in the beautiful Mediterranean, and helped me study Greek women. They also taught me how special they were and how fortunate I am. They survived our adventure and grew into beautiful young women with wonderful families, an abundance of love, and great smiles. This book and my career as a corporate anthropologist could not have happened without their love, support, and their really big hugs when I was most lost on this journey.

To one and all, I sincerely wish to say thank you.

—Andi

SUGGESTED READING

WHILE THERE IS no shortage of reading on innovation or business change management, and there is a growing body of great books on corporate or business anthropology, my suggested reading reflects what I think CEOs, key management, and aspiring managers ought to have on their bookshelf.

Abrams, Bill. *The Observational Research Handbook: Understanding How Consumers Live With Your Product.* Chicago: NTC Business Books with American Marketing Association, 2000.

Ariely, Dan. *Predictably Irrational: The Hidden Forces That Shape Our Decisions.* New York: HarperCollins Publishers, 2008.

Cameron, Kim S. and Robert E. Quinn. *Diagnosing and Changing Organizational Culture.* San Francisco: John Wiley and Sons, Inc., 2006.

Cefkin, Melissa. *Ethnography and the Corporate Encounter.* New York: Berghahn Books, 2009.

Christensen, Clayton M. *The Innovator's Dilemma.* Boston: Harvard Business School Press, 1997.

Christensen, Clayton M. and Henry J. Eyring. *The Innovative University.* San Francisco: Jossey-Bass, 2011.

Christensen, Clayton M., Scott D. Anthony and Erika A. Roth. *Seeing What's Next.* Boston: Harvard Business School Publishing Corporation, 2004.

Duhigg, Charles. *The Power of Habit: Why We Do What We Do In Life and Business.* New York: Random House, 2012.

Halligan, Brian and Dharmesh Shah. *Inbound Marketing: Attract, Engage and Delight Customers Online.* Hoboken: John Wiley and Sons, 2014.

Hurst, Mark and Phil Terry. *Customers Included.* New York: Creative Good Inc., 2013.

Johansson, Frans. *The Medici Effect: Breakthrough Insights at the Intersection of Ideas, Concepts and Cultures.* Boston: Harvard Business School Press, 2004.

Johansson, Frans. *The Click Moment: Seizing Opportunity in an Unpredictable World.* New York: Penguin Group, 2012.

Jordan, Ann T. *Business Anthropology.* Long Grove: Waveland Press, 2003.

Kim, W. Chan and Renée Mauborgne. *Blue Ocean Strategy: How to Create Uncontested Market Space and Make the Competition Irrelevant.* Boston: Harvard Business School Publishing Corporation, 2015.

Ladner, Sam. *Practical Ethnography: A Guide to Doing Ethnography in the Private Sector.* Walnut Creek: Left Coast Press, 2014.

McCracken, Grant. *Chief Culture Officer: How to Create a Living, Breathing Corporation.* New York: Basic Books, 2009.

McCracken, Grant. *Flock and Flow: Predicting and Managing Change in a Dynamic Marketplace.* Bloomington: Indiana University Press, 2006.

McGrath, Rita Gunter. *The End of Competitive Advantage: How to Keep your Strategy Moving as Fast as Your Business*. Boston: Harvard Business School Publishing, 2013.

Raphael, D.D. *The Impartial Spectator: Adam Smith's Moral Philosophy*. Oxford: Oxford University Press, 2007.

Sunderland, Patricia L. and Rita M. Denny. *Doing Anthropology in Consumer Research*. Walnut Creek: Left Coast Press, 2007.

Want, Jerome. *Corporate Culture: Key Strategies of High-Performing Business Cultures*. New York: Saint Martin's Press, 2006.

Underhill, Paco. *Why We Buy: The Science of Shopping*. New York: Simon and Schuster, 1999.

AUTHOR Q & A

Q: The accomplishment of writing your first book must be very grati-fying. Can you discuss some of the joys and challenges of this experi-ence and how it now feels to be an author?

AJS: Becoming an author was never a role I thought about seeking for myself. Yet, now that the book is done and I can add author to my name, I am delighted by the part it plays in who I am, what I have done, and why it matters.

In fact, the book took a number of years, several iterations, and a lot of writing. As I captured my notes for each client, I realized that those notes were the elements of their story. But transforming the elements didn't come easily. They were merely data points, and my job was to find a way to tie them together so that others would enjoy reading about them. The writing of the stories was completely different from the research itself. Writing took much longer and required me to craft every story with perfect attention to detail and in a way that could be enjoyed by and be relevant to the reader.

I learned two things early in the process. The first is that authoring a book is a team sport. Editors—whether they are developmental editors, copy editors, or proofreaders—all played an exceedingly important role in taking what I wrote and making it work much better than I could have on my own. The second is that writing is essential to organizing thoughts into a coher-ent story. Telling a story is one thing; writing it makes it come together in much better ways than the telling of it alone can do.

So why does the book matter? People are storytellers, and storytelling is how we have always captured the history of our lives and shared our values and beliefs. It's how we have shared what gives our lives meaning and purpose. When I first started to pull material together for *On the Brink*, I was intrigued by my clients and their challenges. They had great stories that could be shared with others. I wanted to be the one to tell these stories so that others would not fall into the same traps that my clients had.

Q: The enduring sense of On the Brink *is one of optimism. It's a very positive book and, by extension, it would seem that you are a very optimistic person. Can you share your view of optimism and how it relates to what you do for companies that are "on the brink"?*

AJS: Is your cup half-full or half-empty? Anthropologists love to discover, tinker, try, and play with ideas. We know that the more ideas you have, the more likely you will have big ones in the mix. You may just not immediately know which ones they are. I knew that if I believed in possibilities, I would see opportunities. When I was an executive in large companies, trying to adapt to changing times, I was confronted with challenges all around me. I realized early on that facing these challenges placed me on the journey of the cup half-full. The cup was never completely full— and that was the joyful part! I was always searching for the rest of the cup, and I want others to see their cups as half-full, too.

Q: Can you discuss how you became aware of corporate anthropology and what specific event(s) or revelation(s) led you to move from traditional to corporate anthropology?

AJS: I spent the first decade of my career as a professional academic. That life was very enlightening and I was doing great classic anthropology. But when I went to work at Citibank at the beginning of the deregulation of the banking industry, I realized how powerful the theory, method, and tools of anthropology could be in a business environment, particularly as we worked to change cultures and grow into new market space. We saw very quickly that the well-established management needed to see, feel, and think in new ways or they would not be able to transform their institutions or respond to the new world they were entering. Given all this, it was not hard to apply anthropology in new settings. What *was* hard was hanging that PhD shingle on the door and having the Citibank people understand that if they were to move their culture and the organization forward, how I thought and what I believed mattered.

Q: What are the qualities essential to corporate leaders whose companies are in crisis that can empower them to reach success?

AJS: Humans have always survived by responding to crises by either fleeing or fighting. But neither the ostrich with its head in the ground nor the octopus throwing its arms in every direction is useful when times are changing as they are today. Well before a company faces a crisis, leaders must develop the skills of continuous transformation and learn how to embrace change; they must listen with a new appreciation for ways their own employees and customers might be seeing things that can open doors to tremendous opportunities. I often start a workshop by asking participants to say two things: "Yes, and . . ." and "That's a great idea." What these two phrases do is stop the brain from fighting change and open the mind to new possibilities. For corporate leaders to successfully embrace change, they need to become curious, be willing to test ideas, and empower their staff to try the unfamiliar to deliver innovative solutions—even if those solutions don't always work out as planned.

Q: On the Brink is all about solving problems, and it seems that you are an innate problem-solver. Can you give your impressions of the nature of problem-solving and why you gravitate toward it?

AJS: I have always thought of myself as a Curious George or an amateur explorer. I went into anthropology because I was captivated by different cultures and how people had so many creative ways to solve similar problems. It wasn't hard to embrace the problem-solving approach of ethnography and observational research. Applying the method and tools to the problems of business came naturally as I began to see how hard it was for people to change. I am always happiest in environments where there is a gap or a vacuum between what is and what is becoming. It is more interesting to create the future than to rely on the so-called certainties of the past.

Q: Can you give us some insight into the difficulty or ease with which businesses and executives have been willing to accept and relate to the science of anthropology in solving problems, as opposed to techniques traditionally employed by other types of consultants?

AJS: By and large, no one has ever hired me because I was an anthropologist. At the time, few really understood what I was doing or what I was teaching them to do for themselves. I've always thought the TV series *Undercover Boss* is my best advertising, because it shows people how and why observational research—and particularly participant observation—can focus a very clear lens on the problems of their business without giving the method an academic-sounding name. When compared to other types of qualitative research—focus groups, for example—I have at times had resistance to conducting observational approaches. It can be seen as too long a process and too amorphous, yet it is appreciated once it is understood. My job is always to find meaning in what people are doing or not doing. When presented in layperson's terms as "I am going to help you see, feel, and think in new ways," it is never hard to get a CEO, the management team, and the staff to open up a broad swath where we can go exploring. At Simon Associates Management Consultants, we urge them not to outsource their eyes but to come with us as we go out to find new answers to their core problems.

Q: In On the Brink, *you discuss the intriguing concept of creating a crisis in a healthy company in order to harness the same energy that exists in the midst of a true crisis. Can you expand on this notion of a positive crisis?*

AJS: I believe that some people can anticipate change and lead their teams forward while others keep waiting for the world to return to the way it was. The speed of change today has transformed the entire business landscape so that the life cycle of ideas and products has been reduced to moments. The time between when you come up with a big idea and someone else launches a better one has shrunk from years to maybe months.

With that as the stage for today's business environment, leaders need to stay on their toes and be continuously asking: How many ideas are in their pipelines; who is minding their blogs, Instagram posts, and Twitter feeds; and where will the next challenges come from? Even being the "best of the rest" is no longer a competitive advantage. As Rita McGrath wrote in her book *The End of Competitive Advantage*, the old model where you carved out a space and protected it from the rest is long gone. It's not the space you own today; it's the one you are creating for tomorrow. Every move you make today is setting you up for what's coming your way tomorrow—literally *tomorrow*. The energy that comes from a crisis is like the two-minute drill in football. You just move fast, execute, and keep throwing the ball.

Q: Can you talk about a period in your life when you knew it was time to muster the courage to make a major change, either personally or professionally?

AJS: On September 11, 2001, I was an executive at a medical center in New Jersey. From its rooftop, we watched the World Trade Center towers collapse. Then we spent all night answering the phones in the command center, as people searched for loved ones. It was during that experience that I realized it was time for me to move out on my own and away from a structured corporate environment into the world of an entrepreneur, which is really where I feel most at home. This was both a personal and a professional moment. How lucky I was to find John Rosica, from Rosica Communications, who said, "Andi, you're a corporate anthropologist who helps companies change." It was then that Simon Associates Management Consultants was launched, and I realized my purpose and my personal calling.

Q: Who has been an influence or a source of inspiration in your life and how has this person changed you, your ideas, your goals and visions, or your beliefs about life and success?

AJS: Three major sources of inspiration stand fresh in my mind as I approach each day and each personal and business challenge.

First is my mother, who was a smart, loving, and professional woman. I always marveled at everything she accomplished. She was the youngest of six children whose parents emigrated from Russia to England and finally to New York, where they made a living as a glazer and a seamstress. My parents married right before World War II and my father was sent to the Pacific. My mother spent the war working in her mother-in-law's store in Manhattan. After the war, my mother and father took over running the store and grew it in size and scope. I remember their dinner conversations as part of my training ground. There were endless discussions about how to run the business, manage the help, buy better and smarter, outsmart the competition, and leverage what they had going for them. By the time I was five, I was helping in the store putting clothes on hangers in the basement. Although my father was a very smart man, it was my mother I watched, listened to, and emulated. She was just so very intuitive and intelligent. She made dinner into a time of great learning for me and inspired me to pursue my own passions, experiment with ideas, and debate those ideas without worrying if I were winning or losing on any issue. Although I had been groomed to run the business, I chose a different path. My mother always said to me, "I don't care about what your friends or others are doing; I care only about what you are doing. Think on your own and you will be fine."

Second is my husband. Andy is one cool guy and always my best friend. As a serial entrepreneur, he has built several businesses very successfully. I will always remember his patience and encouragement, along with those all-night walk-around-the-house sessions, as we tried to figure out how to solve his, and then my own, business problems.

Third is John F. Kennedy. While so many of his words were instrumental in my own life as we grew up in the tumultuous

1960s, one favorite is, "Change is the law of life. And those who look only to the past or present are certain to miss the future." That has really been the creed for how I have lived my life.

Q: Discuss a time when something didn't work out as you had wished, and how you overcame disappointment. Also, what do you feel is your greatest career accomplishment up to now?

AJS: I feel rather blessed to have been able to have more joy than not in both my personal life and my professional career. The one thing that didn't work out as I had imagined was my being hired as the president of a midsize commercial bank by the then-president. It soon became apparent that there wasn't room for both of us within the company, so I departed. I was disappointed, to say the least, especially as I had worked hard restoring the institution's financial condition, operating systems, and compliance mechanisms. But forward I went, only to find better opportunities among some fantastic people. What I totally enjoy now is having built a business from scratch, and while that accomplishment is rather special, my real joy is in the team of people working with us. They are just the very best people. That is really all that has mattered. Finding great talent, helping them grow, finding great clients to work with, and then doing it all over again—that is what I thrive on.

Q: Can you talk about the role of serendipity in the search for solutions when companies are faltering?

AJS: The lessons presented in *On the Brink* offer us a great metaphor for the possibilities that surround people inside or outside of companies. While we think it is serendipity, it may be less chance and more the need for a curious mind. I am endlessly fascinated by the difficulty people have in seeing what is all around them, but I know how the brain works and why it is so difficult. Yet, each time a person sees something for the first time, I smile, sit back, and watch their brains change. Those epiphanies are real. We just have to find them. I do believe that the companies that are changing our world today don't let their brains get in the way of seeing those possibilities—and they don't fear failure. The possibilities *are* all around you. Marcel Proust said it so well: "The real voyage of discovery is not in seeking new landscapes, but in having new eyes."

Q: Finally, if you could name the single most significant concept or piece of information you hope your readers will take away after reading On the Brink, *what would it be and why?*

AJS: Change is pain. But the pain you feel today is the strength you will have tomorrow. As John Quincy Adams said, "If your actions inspire others to dream more, learn more, do more, and become more, then you are a leader." Lead on!

ABOUT THE AUTHOR

ANDREA SIMON, "ANDI," is a corporate anthropologist who specializes in working with organizations that need or want to change. Her company, Simon Associates Management Consultants (SAMC), applies the theories, methods, and tools of corporate anthropology and ethnographic research to businesses and not-for-profit organizations. Dr. Simon formed SAMC to help companies and organizations adapt to changing times. Her proprietary ChangeMap™ process enables companies to envision a future and then "reverse plan" to ensure that the vision is achievable.

Prior to opening her consulting business in 2002, Dr. Simon held executive management positions in financial services and health-care organizations. She was executive vice president of First National Bank of Highland and senior vice president of Poughkeepsie Savings Banks, and held management and consulting roles at Citibank. She spent seven years as a health-care executive, during which she set up branding and marketing for Montefiore Medical Center, and was vice president of branding, marketing, and culture change for St. Joseph's Regional Medical Center.

Dr. Simon has a BA from Pennsylvania State University and a PhD from City University of New York. She has been on the faculty of higher education institutions, including Ramapo College of New Jersey, where she was a tenured professor of anthropology and American studies, and Washington

170 ON THE BRINK

University in St. Louis, where she was a visiting professor teaching entrepreneurship to arts and science students.

She is a trained practitioner in Blue Ocean Strategy and since 2007, has given over 250 CEO workshops and speeches on the topic and consulted with a wide range of clients to help them redesign their strategies and open new markets.

Dr. Simon is also highly experienced in culture change methodologies, particularly the use of the Organizational Culture Assessment Instrument (OCAI), which was developed at the University of Michigan. An Innovation Games® facilitator and trainer, Dr. Simon has conducted Innovation Games with dozens of clients and uses Innovation Games and Serious Play methods when working with clients on culture change and innovation challenges.

Dr. Simon has appeared on *Good Morning America* and has been interviewed for *The Washington Post*, *Business Week*, and *Forbes*, and has written for *FierceHealthcare*, *Executive Street* blog, and *American Banker*, among other blogs and publications. A widely engaged speaker, she has conducted workshops and speeches for organizations such as Vistage International, TEC, and The Executive Council, and has presented keynote speeches and workshops at the National Association of Electrical Distributors, Family Firm Institute, IACC, ABIT, Society for Healthcare Strategy and Market Development, and the Forum for Healthcare Marketing, among others.